Irene Alexander lives in Brisbane, Aus
of Social Sciences at Christian Herit
larly interested in the integration of spirituality, psychology and
everyday life.

Born in New Zealand, Irene has lived in several other countries. She is the mother of two adult sons.

DANCING WITH GOD

Transformation through relationship

Irene Alexander

First published in Great Britain in 2007

Society for Promoting Christian Knowledge
36 Causton Street
London SW1P 4ST

British Library Cataloguing-in-Publication Data
A catalogue record for this book is available from the British Library

ISBN 978–0–281–05965–2

1 3 5 7 9 10 8 6 4 2

Typeset by Graphicraft Ltd, Hong Kong
Printed in Great Britain by Ashford Colour Press

Produced on paper from sustainable forests

*With gratitude to Christian Heritage College
for giving me the time to write
and to the Rivendell Community
for giving me the place*

Contents

Introduction

The mystery that we call God wants to dance.
It is evident in the thistledown on the wind.
The swallows in the evening light.
In the leaves and branches of trees at the lightest touch of a breeze.
In the sunlight dancing on the water.
At the lift of our hearts hearing music.
And children's instinctive enjoyment of movement.
And even our feet tapping a rhythm – calling our bodies to rise and join in.
The beauty of ballet and other dancing that somehow says to our hearts – this is what you were made for.

In Ladinsky's versions of the songs of the Persian mystic Shams-ud-din Muhammad Hafiz, he calls God the one who only knows four words:

Every
Child
Has known God.
Not the God of names,
Not the God of don'ts,
Not the God who ever does
Anything weird,
But the God who only knows four words
And keeps repeating them, saying:
'Come dance with Me.'
Come
Dance.[1]

Not being very musical, I have to talk my way through any formal dance steps – 'Right foot first. Back, side, together' – over and over. Other people seem to just get out on the dance floor and let the music take them. I did have one experience of

dancing being easy, effortless, natural. As teenagers we were
having dance lessons. The instructor would demonstrate a step,
partnering each of us. He would hold his hip against ours and
lead with his body. Suddenly I could do it. If I leant my hip
against his I could feel where his body was going and simply
flow with it. Years later, I remembered this experience. I was
thinking about Jesus' words, 'Come to me, all who labour and
are heavy laden, and I will give you rest. Take my yoke upon you
and learn from me; for I am gentle and lowly in heart, and
you will find rest for your souls. For my yoke is easy, and my
burden is light.'[2] I was considering how we all know what a yoke
is and can imagine what Jesus meant about being in a yoke with
him. Still, it is not an everyday experience for us as it would have
been for many of Jesus' listeners. As I imagined the experience
of learning from Jesus' movements, the memory of this dancing
experience returned. What if Jesus had said to us, 'Come to me
all of you who are having difficulty finding the rhythms of grace.
Place your hip on mine. Lean into me and the rhythm will flow.
You will dance in simplicity and humility, as you were created
to do.' Ah, yes, learning to dance with the Creator is how we are
called to life.

Being human we often make hard going of it. We make the
same mistakes over and over or, having mastered one step, forget the one we learned before or else simply don't understand
how to go with the flow of the universe.

This book is an exploration of some of the ways to dance that
I have found and some of the obstacles that hinder my dancing.

1

The beginning of the story . . .

---◆◆◆---

Once upon a time, in a far away land, a long time ago – or maybe not so far away and not so long ago – lived a young man and a young woman. They were in love. They hoped, desperately, that they could get married, but they lived in a country and a time where the girl's parents arranged her marriage and being in love was not considered the most important factor in what was regarded as a suitable agreement. The girl's father wanted a much better arrangement for her than that. He wanted someone rich so her future comfort and security would be guaranteed and this boy, he was only a merchant's son with his fortune still to be made. The girl had begged her father – as much as she had been able – but, when she saw that it was only making him more determined to refuse to agree, she had to keep silent.

She really hardly knew her beloved – it was not done for a young man and woman to meet and talk. The only reason she had ever been able to be with him was because her maid, with whom she had grown up and shared all her secrets, had been able to arrange some brief encounters for her. When they occasionally met in public, their eyes spoke volumes. In spite of having only these snatched moments to draw on, she knew he was the one for her and longed with all her heart to be with him.

Maybe the secret encounters were found out. Maybe the parents of both agreed it was not a suitable partnership. Who knows, but one day the maid came with the awful news that he was to be sent away. His father was sending him on a trading venture – he was to travel to the East and see what contacts he could set up, what goods he could arrange to purchase. He would be gone a long time. Maybe for ever. She knew that her parents would be relieved and expect her to get over him, but her heart was nearly broken. Somehow the maid managed to arrange a last meeting for them before he left. They told each other of their

1

love, their hope for a future together – maybe he would become rich and famous and could come back for her. It could not be that he would never come back at all.

She heard through her maid when he left the country and then they heard nothing of him for weeks, for months, for a year.

Meantime her father looked out for other possible husbands for her. One day her mother came to her and told her of a planned meeting with a possible suitor. She had learned by now to hide her feelings and she politely asked about him, knowing that's what her mother would expect. Well, he was very rich. He was a widower. He and his wife had had no children. He was an older man who hoped to take a young wife to be with him in his old age and hopefully produce an heir to inherit his wealth. Yes, he was a lot older than they had planned, but he was very kind and he would give her a secure future. The girl did not dare show her reaction – what was the use and, anyway, if her beloved never came back, who was to say that this would not be better than other possibilities. So she submitted to the meeting – and obviously met with his approval. Wedding plans were made and she tried to find some sparks of interest. Her parents put her quietness down to normal anxiety about such a change in her life. At the same time, the maid tried to find out if there was any word about her mistress' real love, but came back with nothing. Nothing had been heard. Such were the times that it was possible he was dead or that, eventually, a message would get through. Nobody knew.

The wedding went ahead. She moved to her husband's mansion and, indeed, it was a change in her life. She had to learn how the household ran, but, really, it ran very well without any input from her. There were servants to do everything. There was even discussion about whether her own maid needed to come with her, but, in the end, she was allowed to come. The young bride tried to learn what she could about how the household ran and to please her new husband. Indeed she did please him. He was delighted to have a companion again and a young bride in his bed. He did not expect much of her and knew so little about her that he would not be able to tell how much of herself she kept hidden from him and from the eyes of his servants. His personal servant, who considered her an intrusion, watched for any behaviour he considered unacceptable. Fortunately, his complaints to his master were not heeded, but, still, it was an irritation to her to know that he watched every time she ventured out to the market and told her husband what she did. She finally realized that the servant was jealous of her special standing in a household that had been running very smoothly under his control for a long time. She tried to avoid him, even please him, but still she knew his watchful eyes were upon her.

The months passed. To everyone's delight, she became pregnant. When a boy was born, she knew that her husband's dream had been fulfilled. The servants looked after the child and she tried to be as good a mother to him as she could. Then, one day, her maid came in from the market with such a look on her face that she knew something exciting must have happened. As soon as she could, she found a way to be alone with her. 'They've had a message! He's coming home!' She hadn't been able to find out too many details without arousing people's suspicion, but she'd heard the talk – he had traded successfully, set up some kind of trade agreement, was going to be back with rare purchases from the East. Oh, to know that he was safe and alive! She and the maid laughed and cried together.

For some time she heard nothing, but every time she thought of him her heart beat faster. She realized how much more she was smiling when her husband, who noticed little of what she did, commented one day that motherhood obviously suited her. She tried to hide her happiness, but every time the maid came back with some little snippet of news it would set her heart singing.

Finally, one day the news came through that he was home. He had been successful. They were preparing a celebration for his homecoming. If only she could go. If only she could just see him again, even from a distance. It was impossible. Her husband mixed in other circles. A wife did not have friends or interests of her own. At least he was back. At least he was nearby. She tried to be content with that. Only her maid knew how much she longed to see him.

Life went on. The child was growing. Her husband was content with his interests. The life of the household flowed in its daily rhythm. She would go to the markets and various community events. The maid brought back news from the outside world that helped keep her a little in touch with others' lives.

Then, one day, the maid had that look in her eyes again. The look of a secret just bursting to be shared. 'I met him! He was down in the markets and what a man he has become. He asked

3

after you the moment he realized who I was. He even managed to whisper to me that he would love to see you, but then we were interrupted. I'm sure he'll look for me again, though.'

Surely something could be arranged. Just a few minutes together, just to see him again – that would be enough. They both had their own lives, but to meet his eyes, maybe touch his hand. Eventually the maid worked it out. In the home of one of his friends, the entrance off a little alley. She could slip in and be with him for a few minutes on one of her visits to the market. Oh, just to see him again!

So they met and it was as though they had never been apart, except that now they knew so much more about life. She wanted to hear what he had done, what he had seen. It seemed as if she could have poured out her heart to him, but so little time. She tried to convince herself that it was enough. It was enough to have seen him. It was enough to see what a man he had become. She said goodbye and tried to believe that she was content, that now she could wish him well for his life and hers would go on. As the days passed, though, the old grief returned, the 'if onlys' of her previous longing. She asked the maid if maybe they could meet just one more time.

So it went on. She would tell herself that it would only be once more. They would meet and both vow that this was the last time. She would try not to ask her maid for news and scare herself with imagining her husband finding out, but then she would give in and work out how to see him. They would touch and she knew how very different it would be if she was with him. She would tell herself it could not be and try to immerse herself in her husband's life. She would play with her son and try to be a perfect mother.

Then, one day, the maid came and told her that he was planning another trip. Again, he would be away for an extended period. Surely just one more meeting to say goodbye.

It was arranged. It seemed perfect. Her husband was out for the day, his servant with him. Nothing was expected of her. The child was cared for. She could have an extended time with him. One last time, then it would be over.

They met and talked and held each other and somehow this last time it seemed as if they really could be lovers before saying goodbye for ever. He was so loving, so understanding, so different from her husband. As they lay together, she began to wonder if after all they couldn't work something out. Could she somehow come to him in another land?

4

Then, the door burst open and her worst fears were realized. There was her husband's servant, with other men, and they dragged her away, screaming abuse at her.

She was thrown into an underground room, the door locked and barred. She spent the night weeping. It was likely that she would be killed – the penalty for her betrayal. In a way she welcomed it. How could she ever go back to her husband after what she had done, after betraying his trust and kindness? How would she possibly live there, with the servant's eyes on her – all his suspicions proven. Anyway, her husband probably would not take her back, having shamed him as she had. He would keep her son, too, no question. How could she bear to live without her son? Would her father take her back? She had shamed him, too. He would not be able to find her another husband even if he did take her back. She would become as a servant at the very best. Perhaps they would not have her. Maybe she would even have to become a prostitute to stay alive. She played through the scenarios. In reality, how could her lover even have her? He relied totally on his father for the trade he was setting up. His father would not approve of her for an instant. It was unlikely anything could happen between them. They would come for her in the morning. They would drag her through the streets half naked to show what a shameful woman she was and then they would stone her to death. Oh God, what had she done? God. How could she stand before God? Of course she knew that what she had done was wrong. She had tried to stop, tried to justify to herself that God would understand, but now she faced it squarely. God's law was very clear, she was an adulteress and worthy only of death – God would not pardon her. In either life or death, there was no hope for her.

The night dragged on. She huddled in a corner and began to think of what it would be like for each of the others in her life. Her son, with such a sinful mother. Her husband, bereft of a wife again. Her parents, shamed and grieved. Her lover, tainted forever. Her maid, probably cast out on to the street. Her tears began again. She pleaded with God to somehow care for those she was leaving, to somehow make it up to them. As she wept, she felt some measure of God's comfort, some memory of sacred writings that said God was a merciful God to those whose hearts were broken and contrite.

In the morning, they came for her. The jealous servant was among them, identifying her as the guilty one. It was as she had known it would be. She was dragged through the streets and brought before the religious leaders for their verdict. She let her long hair fall around her face so she would see as little as possible, but she could still hear the jeers of the crowd, recognize the streets as they came near the temple, see the stones in the hands of some of those gathering to join in. Then she was thrown down and the accusation shouted out above her: 'We caught her in the very act of adultery. The law says that she should be stoned.' She almost expected the stones to start immediately as she lay huddled on the ground, her hair covering her face, but the noise of the crowd slowly quieted and even the scuffling of feet stopped. Through her hair she could see a figure stooped, doing something on the ground. The accusation came again: 'She committed adultery. What do you say about her?' Again she could see the figure stooped and writing with his finger on the ground. She could sense the puzzlement of the crowd, the impatience of the religious ones. Obviously this man was some kind of authority, but he was stooping down beside her. She could almost feel the power play going on around her.

Then a voice, authoritative and yet quiet and steady: 'Let him who is without sin among you be the first to throw a stone at her.' She tensed, waiting for a stone. Nothing. Silence. 'Him who is without sin.' She knew that the religious leaders would put themselves in that category. Even her husband's servant would see himself as that. Righteous – self-righteous, any hint of sin hidden. The silence continued and she could see him bent, writing on the ground with his finger. She could hear some movement among the crowd and gradually began to realize that they were leaving. Somehow this man was exposing that hidden sin. Somehow they could not stand up to him. She dared to look around her. No one was left except for him. She turned her eyes towards him and saw such intentness as she had never seen in the eyes of a man. Compassion, knowing, nothing hidden. She began to understand why the people could not stand before him. He looked deeply into her and said, 'Woman, where are they? Has no one condemned you?' She looked around again, hardly believing, then back at him – this man who could see into hearts – and said, 'No one, sir.' Jesus said, 'Then neither do I condemn you; go now and do not sin again.'[1]

I imagine the woman getting up, wondering how to start her life again. Where did she go and how was it for her? Whatever she did, I believe that she never forgot those eyes and the words 'neither do I condemn you' for there is the good news in one sentence, that God says 'neither do I condemn you.'

I imagine Jesus standing in the temple courtyard looking towards the hill of Golgotha, the place of the skull, and, in his mind's eye, seeing a cross set up there, knowing that his morning's words had cost him dearly. The Pharisees would not forgive him for this. Not only had he set aside the imposition of a legal punishment but he had also exposed their own sin.

What about the woman? She got off scot-free. Jesus went to his death in her place. She, of course, is me – and each one of us who has ever done wrong and seen our wrongdoing and come before the God who sees our hearts. Here is a God I can dance with!

2

The inner life – the kingdom within

I don't believe that Jesus came to start a new religion. He came into the midst of an existing religion and was faithful to that religion. In fact, he made it clear that he had not come to abolish the 'law or the prophets' and neither should others,[1] yet seemed to be challenging that religion and the religious leaders all the time. The story of the woman found in adultery is just such an example. What he did meant that she did not receive the punishment that the law declared to be just. In the end, he was killed for repeatedly acting in this way, so what was he doing?

He was doing something much deeper than the religious laws could hope to achieve. In some ways I don't think that it would have mattered which religion Jesus was born into – in the sense that he was upholding the good in Judaism (the 'law and the prophets'), but it could easily have been the good in any other religion – he would have done the same thing. He probed beneath all the religious practices and interpretations and looked at the heart, telling of the kingdom within, the kingdom of heaven. That is what he talked about all the time. 'The kingdom of heaven is like . . .' In parable after parable, teaching after teaching, he showed us what the kingdom is like – a treasure hidden in a field, a father who welcomes an undeserving son, a vineyard owner who gives more than is fair to the labourers, a feast to which those from the highways and byways are welcomed, a place that is open to the poor in spirit, the broken and sinners. It seems that much of this teaching is about a kingdom that can be visible – a quality of relationships where the poor are ministered to, people show love to each other and each person can be accepted and receive God's love.

He also said, however, 'My kingdom is not of this world.'[2] Some people think that this means Jesus was talking about what happens after we die – that we will go and live in heaven – and this has certainly been a dominant focus for Christians, but he also seemed exceedingly concerned about how we live now, while we are still alive. Thus, he was talking about not being a part of this world's systems and ways of thinking. He was speaking of a spiritual kingdom – one that, indeed, engenders visible results, but is initially and primarily an inner place, the kingdom within.

Certainly, Jesus' teaching shows us the possibility of a kingdom without – a kingdom where people are ministered to. Much of his teaching has clear outward results, such as healing the sick, giving to the poor, setting free the oppressed, welcoming in the marginalized. However, that visible kingdom is the result of an inner relationship, an inner responsiveness to God, and some of his teaching clearly speaks to an inner reality rather than an outer one: 'Take the log out of your own eye, and then you will see clearly to take the speck out of your brother's eye.'[3] What can this mean but that we need to attend to our own hearts' secrets, our own weaknesses, before we try to correct each others'. Proverbs tells us to 'keep your heart with all vigilance, for from it flow the springs of life.'[4] What does it mean to guard the heart? Surely it means that we need to be aware of this inner world.

The kingdom of God, then, is the inner kingdom, the place where God is king or, to use a more gender-neutral term, the realm of God – the place where God is sovereign. Language being limited as it is, we have to look for the meaning beneath the words. The point is that Jesus is talking about an alternative way of being in the world. It is a way of being in which the divine mystery that we call God is sovereign. A way of being in which the inner life, the inner realm, is lined up with all that is good and merciful and true. Jesus tries to tell us how to do this. What a task. Our human minds get so caught up in the outer world, the systems we live according to, the ways our culture does things. Already there is a trap that needs to be addressed. It is that, when Jesus speaks of the kingdom, God's realm, he is not just speaking of an other-worldly way of being. He doesn't imply that we need to withdraw from the culture around us. In fact, he actually tells us that we are to be in the world but not of it.[5] Nor does he imply that we should treat the earth as expendable. The original purpose of creation, as the Jews understood it, still stands and our mandate from Genesis 1.28 is to look after the earth – it is the real meaning of the phrase 'to have dominion over' (NRSV). Until more recent decades, many Christians understood this to mean that we should dominate nature rather than nurture it.

So, Jesus has not called us to act as though the physical world does not matter, nor to be separate from the cultures we live in, but, rather, to ensure that our focus, our values and our everyday lives are centred on our relationship with God. We need to choose to live out that mystery in our inner lives and, then, in the lives of those around us. His call to 'seek first his kingdom',[6] is an invitation to first live in an inner world that is aligned with God's love, mercy and justice.

The way to the divine other has more to do with our inner lives than our outward appearance, our outward behaviour. Each person, Christian or not, religious or not, has an inner life. Implicit in the recognition of an inner life is that tending to it involves a search for meaning. For some this is a less conscious search than for others, but all human beings are meaningmakers. Ecclesiastes has it that God has set eternity in our hearts.[7] We are created with a longing for something more. There is a homesickness in our hearts for eternity, for something beyond the drudgery of our everyday lives. Rilke, a German poet, expresses it like this: 'You, the great homesickness we could not overcome; you the forest we could never leave . . .'[8]

How does all this relate to the woman found in adultery? Does it mean that we can live however we want to? That is clearly not what Jesus teaches. What he is emphasizing, over and over, is that it is a matter of the heart, not just outwardly complying with a set of rules. That was his argument with the Pharisees, with any religious system that focuses on outward behaviour but does not change the heart – does not nurture a relationship with the Divine within, that instead develops only an outer veneer, a mask.

John Sanford in *The Kingdom Within*[9] uses the teaching regarding the Pharisees to show the difference between the inner world and the mask that we show to others. Jesus rebuked the Pharisees for their hypocrisy. The word 'hypocrite' means actor and refers to the idea that actors in those days wore a mask depicting the character they were playing. So, a hypocrite was a maskwearer.

The Pharisees were the ultimate maskwearers as they wanted the world to see them as generous, holy, righteous people – that, after all, was their outward behaviour in public. Jesus, however, exposed their inner poverty, their inner sins against the spirit, as being of much more concern to him than even sins of the flesh: 'Woe to you, teachers of the law and Pharisees, you hypocrites! You clean the outside of the cup and dish, but inside they are full of greed and self-indulgence'[10] and 'You are masters at making yourselves look good in front of others, but God knows what's behind the appearance.'[11]

In the story of the woman found in adultery, Jesus' challenge to the crowd was for them to examine their inner lives. He did not argue about whether the woman was guilty or not. He did not get caught up in arguments about the literal meaning or application of the law. He aimed much deeper. What is your inner life like? Are you really any better than she is?

I understand that it was the custom for the oldest person present to throw the first stone. The members of the crowd left gradually because, as each person left standing around her realized that now he was the oldest present, that the onus was on him and he could not say 'I am without sin', he had to leave.

The human condition is imperfection. Living in the kingdom within is a journey towards wholeness and good relationships, including our relationship with the Divine, our dancing with God. It cannot be born out of self-righteousness, but out of a relationship with a God who chooses not to condemn but to welcome: 'neither do I condemn you.'[12] This God, shown to us in Jesus, is one who welcomes, comes looking for those in need. He came from heaven poor[13] in order to find the poor, the needy, the broken.

3

The man with the shrivelled hand

———•◦•———

Shame
for all his life, unable to do things like other people
Always the odd one out.
Always the one people look sideways at.
Always the one suspected of sin.
Was it this man who sinned
or maybe his parents –
that he should have such a deformity?
A hand shrivelled and unusable.[1]
Oh the shame.
What sinners his family must be,
that God has punished them like this.

>   He knew they thought that.
>   Even if they did not say it outright –
>   whispered it to each other,
>   self-righteously compared their wholeness with his
>   brokenness,
>   believing that somehow he was to blame.

He had gone to God
>   over and over.
>   What have I done?
>   What can I repent of?
>   What secret sin have I committed?
>   What secret look given?
>   What secret act committed?
>   God show me that I may repent.
Sometimes there was peace –
>   I have done all I know.
Sometimes there was turmoil –
>   is there yet some hidden thing,
>   some thing unrepented,
>   some pride held?

The man with the shrivelled hand

All his life,
  this secret shame
    for all to see
    in every act.

He expected to carry this burden all his life.
  always depending on others for help.
Giving help with his one good hand when he could.
Still he turned his heart to the living God.
  Still went to the temple on the sabbath.
  Still asked God for cleansing
  and healing – when he dared.

Then he heard a healer had come.
He'd heard of others and sometimes even watched as others
  went home healed,
but not him.
No one could heal a hand that had never formed properly.
No one could take away his shame.

Jesus noticed him.
Somehow among all the crowd he saw him.
How did he do that?
Was he looking for ones such as he?
He who came poor from heaven, did he look for those who
  were broken?
He saw him, and called him forward,
'Come, son of Abraham,
come faithful one.
I am Son of my Father.
I see your heart towards me,
I see your faith.
I see your doubts.
I see you.'

He called him to come, to stand tall for all to see.
He laid his hands on him.
Not for the crowd,
not for the praise,
not for the show.
He sees the little ones.
The bent and broken.
That's what he came for.

He called him forward before them all.
All the crowd.
All the religious leaders.
'Come and stand here.
May I not heal this son of Abraham?'
Jesus touched him
and his hand became whole.

He went home dancing and waving his arms in the air!

Jesus
   was left to argue
      with the religious ones.

Do you not rescue your sheep if it has fallen into a ditch on
   the sabbath?
The sabbath that was made for man, not man for the sabbath.
The sabbath that was made for freedom.

What about him, a son of Abraham, may I not rescue him on
   the sabbath?

Eventually they got him for it.
   Eventually they killed him.
      Ha, you sabbath breaker,
         you who break the rules,
            now you are broken.

He came poor.
   He became broken,
      but he set me free.

4

True self and false self

————◦•◦————

The story of the man with the shrivelled hand shows, again, the contrast between the kingdom of God, the realm of the Divine, and the legalistic, self-righteous way of thinking, the masks, of the religious ones. This theme recurs over and over. The contrast between those who come to God, simply, in a place of need, and those who come trying to prove that they are worthy. Indeed, this is a dominant theme of the human condition – the question as to what true goodness is, what makes us acceptable to a righteous God. What is a good life? What is morality to be measured by? How are our justice systems to evaluate what is acceptable behaviour? How do we truly understand goodness and right living?

Within each one of us, these questions and possible answers are played out, often unconsciously, in the daily choices we make, our understanding of right and wrong, decisions we make that reflect our inner values. These values influence our decisions to do something right, whether anyone knows of it or not, or, in contrast, to create an outer mask, because we care tremendously what people think of us. How these questions are played out, our responses to them and our inner world, result largely from our childhood experiences. This is the foundation of both our inner being and our outward behaviour, much of which continues for our entire lifetime.

From earliest childhood we look to our caregivers for food, warmth, safety and love. We learn how to behave to ensure that our basic needs are met. They are met by those who, to us then, are godlike figures. Godlike because, to a helpless child, parents and caregivers are all-powerful. They have the power to give or withhold everything that we need. So, the smallest child begins to learn 'scripts', as psychologists call them, of how to please those who look after them, how to behave in ways that will get them what they want. Those patterns of behaviour are repeated over and over. Some are even specifically required: 'Mummy won't love you unless you behave', 'Daddy will only bring home presents if you are good'. In this way, most of us learn how to 'be good' – how to fulfil the requirements of the powerful ones in our lives. As we get older, these patterns of 'being good' become our scripts for earning the approval of authority figures in general and, thus, implicitly, of earning the approval of the ultimate authority figure, whether we consciously use the name God or not. The Pharisees in the story of the man with the shrivelled hand give us a picture of this way of living – the continual attempt to live righteously in order to fulfil the requirements of authority.

This process of 'doing the right thing' so that we get what we want (and need), sets up the construct of the 'false self' – the behaviour or practices that we feel, almost instinctively, are the 'right' ways to behave. Even if we rebel against these, we are often rebelling against a standard that we still regard as the ultimate authority – as though we still believe that they are the 'right' ways to behave, despite the fact that we choose to behave differently. The more we practise such behaviour and the more we use these standards to measure our own and others' behaviour, the more entrenched the scripts become. For those of us who manage to 'be good' most of the time, such practices do lead to approval and success, so the false self works fairly well. In fact, though we may think that we are living morally, becoming 'good' people, we are really only building up the ego, developing strong walls of looking good, focusing on the outer mask. Many of us feel that, for a time, we *do* fulfil the necessary conditions, we *do* please God and other people. If we don't feel that, then we try harder, still caught in the paradigm.

Donald Winnicott, the theorist on child psychology who formulated these ideas explains: 'Through this False Self the infant builds up a false set of relationships, by means of introjection even attains a show of being real, so that the child may grow to be just like the mother, nurse, aunt, brother, or whoever dominates the scene. The False Self has one positive and

16

very important function: to hide the True Self, which it does by compliance with environmental demands.'[1]

The false self is formed, then, by fulfilling all the internalized rules and requirements to gain acceptance and approval from those we value – including God. Often we are not even aware that we have transferred these beliefs on to God, yet we spend our time living according to certain internalized patterns of behaviour that we think will gain this God's approval (Figure 1).

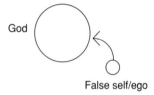

God

False self/ego

Figure 1
Striving from without:
living according to self-made requirements

Most of humankind is caught, to some extent, in this construct of the false self. To put it in other words, we continue with certain behaviour that serves to make us feel acceptable in the dominant paradigm. Most of us do this most of the time, but some people escape from this.

One group of such people is the mystics. They are those rare people who, in some way, seem to see through the common illusions the rest of us live by and somehow find their way to the Divine more deeply and experientially. Daniel Ladinsky draws on the writings of Shams-ud-din Muhammad Hafiz, himself a fourteenth-century Persian mystic, to express it like this:

What is the difference
Between your experience of Existence
And that of a saint?

The saint knows
That the spiritual path
Is a sublime chess game with God.

> And the Beloved
> Has just made such a Fantastic Move
> That the saint is continually
> Tripping over Joy
> And bursting out in Laughter
> And saying 'I surrender!'
>
> Whereas, my dear,
> I am afraid you still think
> You have a thousand serious moves.[2]

Indeed, most of us do still think that we have a thousand serious ways in which we can win the approval of God. The mystics laugh and surrender. They never think to ask the question, 'Am I doing OK?' They understand that it is an irrelevant question. They come to God on the basis of who God is, not on the basis of their own behaviour.

The other group of people who find their way out of the false self trap are the broken ones. The broken ones are the people who look at the idea of getting approval from God by their own efforts and know that they cannot do it. The story of the man with the shrivelled hand shows us this. There is nothing he can do to heal himself and he knows it. Then God, in Jesus, comes looking for him. He looks for the ones who know that they need him. Jesus' story of the prodigal son is a classical illustration of this.[3] The prodigal son knows that he does not deserve to be called son, he just wants to come back to his father. His motives might not have even been very good, but he came in brokenness, admitting his need. The father welcomed him with open arms – in fact, he ran to meet him, would not allow him to finish his speech of repentance, took him in and showered him with blessing. The woman who washed Jesus' feet with her tears was also such a one.[4] She was a 'sinner' – probably a prostitute, going by the way Simon and the others reacted. She braved their criticism and did not act in the way they expected – she simply wept over Jesus' feet and wiped them with her hair.

It is the broken people who more frequently understand the way of the kingdom, knowing that all they can do is throw themselves on the mercy of God – God's mercy, after all, is the only way into the kingdom. The broken ones are most likely to look at all the rules and regulations of the Church and society around them and say, 'I can't do it, I just cannot reach those standards.' As a result, they find the God who says, 'I've done it already. There's nothing you have to do.'

This process highlights for us the way of the 'true self'. Perhaps the best way to identify it is to think of some experience, some time when we have felt deeply loved, deeply accepted by God. For some people this may be their conversion experience, for others some special revelation of love, of knowing, even momentarily, that we are loved just for who we are and for nothing else. That sense of falling into God, falling into God's arms and saying, 'Oh, I get it, I don't actually have to do anything', understanding that it is, after all, all grace. The sense of self in that moment is the closest we can get to the 'true self'. This does not mean that there is only one way to be the true self or that the true self is static, but, rather, it is a discovering with God the person who we are most at home being, most happy with, most 'at one' with. It is about being able to let go of all the striving and rules and regulations, achievements and performance inherited from our childhood (and adulthood) and abandoning ourselves to the Divine.

Author and priest Basil Pennington helps us to identify the true self by comparing it to how we feel when we know that we are loved, in love: 'One of the great experiences of life is that first experience of being in love and being loved. Of course our parents love us. They have to, or so it seems, and siblings, too. But the first time someone loves us for no other reason than that person has in some way perceived our true beauty, our true lovableness, we float. We are ecstatic. For we have seen in the eyes of the lover something of our own true beauty. The only way we really see ourselves is when we see ourselves reflected back to us from the eyes of one who truly loves us.'[5] Further, 'When we perceive more and more clearly our true self in God, we are all but dazzled by the wonder of this image of God. But at the same time we are profoundly humbled. For we know that we are made in the image and likeness of God . . . And we know that, but for the grace of God, it could be wholly lost.'[6] It is the love of God that first reflects to us the image of the true self and it is the grace of God that keeps us in the place of ceasing our striving and, instead, letting our hearts simply open to the God of grace, rather than creating images of God that require correct subservience. Rainer Maria Rilke understood this imaging of the Divine:

> O you brooding darkness from which the first morning
>   dawned,
> We must not, of our own doing,
> paint you with the same lines and images
> with which the holy men concealed you.
>
> We create images of you like screens
> so already a thousand walls surround you.
> And when our hearts open with longing
> our pious hands hide you.[7]

Rilke recognizes that the way to the Divine is in the simple opening of our hearts – our busy serving and doing often only hides the very one we seek. The mystics, then, and the broken ones find their way most easily to the true self. The part of myself that is 'whole', 'together', performing and achieving and looking good can actually keep me in the ego, behind the mask of the false self, the self that Jesus told us that we need to die to.

Coming to this place of the true self is most commonly achieved when we experience failure or brokenness because then the hard shell of ego and false self is broken. The man with the shrivelled hand creates a picture of this for us. He is one who knows that he is in need. He is one who knows that there is nothing more he can do. As a result, he is one who discovers the God who comes looking for him. The prodigal is no longer the popular rich boy; he is a much humbler figure. The woman who washed Jesus' feet with her tears, looked down on by society, is acceptable to God and knows herself loved and valued. She is free to give love in return – more so than the critical, self-righteous onlookers. This indeed is the key. The false self is in some way self-righteous, whereas the true self is resting in God's arms, not even thinking about righteousness (Figure 2).

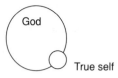

Figure 2
Resting in God: abiding in relationship

What these stories show us is that the broken part of us – the place where we feel most a failure or a sinner – is often the part that will lead us to finding that God is a God of grace. It is that part of us that will lead us home, back to the arms of the waiting God. If I can stay with it, if I can recognize and accept my brokenness and stay there, and so find the acceptance of the Divine, then I can find my true self. Most of us have been schooled to hide this part, even to hide it from ourselves, to turn away from it as quickly as we can. This is very different from a discovery of the true self, the self that does not have to strive for acceptance, that does not have to perform to gain approval, the self that can just be.

In Luke 18, Jesus tells a wonderful parable of the true self and the false self 'to some who were confident of their own righteousness and looked down on everybody else.'[8] He told the story to those who lived in the place of the false self or, in Eugene Peterson's words, 'to some who were complacently pleased with themselves over their moral performance'[9] – the Pharisees.

> Two men went up to the temple to pray, one a Pharisee and the other a tax collector. The Pharisee stood up and prayed about himself: 'God, I thank you that I am not like other men – robbers, evildoers, adulterers – or even like this tax collector. I fast twice a week and give a tenth of all I get.'
>
> But the tax collector stood at a distance. He would not even look up to heaven, but beat his breast and said, 'God, have mercy on me, a sinner.'[10]

Jesus' evaluation of these 'moral' positions was that it was the taxman, not the other, who went home *made right* with God: 'I tell you that this man, rather than the other, went home justified before God.'[11] It was the taxman, the failing one, the broken one, whose very weakness brought him into the presence of God. The

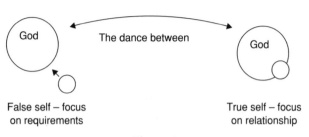

Figure 3
The dance between the true self and the false self

'others' of us, the good ones, may wrestle back and forth with fulfilling the requirements and then praise ourselves for so doing. Jesus does not commend this way of being: 'You are masters at making yourselves look good in front of others, but God knows what's behind the appearance.'[12]

The reality is that most of us live the majority of the time in the false self, trying to be virtuous. Most of us strive to be accepted and evaluate our performance over and over each day. Living in the kingdom is learning to live more frequently in the place of the true self, in the place of being who we are, freely and joyfully. It is learning to recognize more frequently when we are living out of the false self, so that we can choose those practices that lead us into God's presence and allow us to live freely in our true self (Figure 3).

So, there is a dance between the true self and the false self, a moving back and forth between them, but, hopefully, a gradual learning to stay more often in the true self, the presence of God. We may find ourselves in the true self – that place where we know ourselves truly loved – and then something will happen, maybe to do with our work or our need for approval or our desire for love, and we dance back over to trying to fulfil all the requirements again, to try and impress God, to try and impress other people. Hopefully, more and more, we will be able to catch ourselves when we do that and be able to say, 'No. God, it is your grace. I just want to find myself in your embrace.' So we dance. It is a fact of our lives, that we go back and forth between the false self, seeking approval, damning ourselves for falling short, and the true self – the self that Jesus says is worth more than the whole world, the self that simply abandons itself to the grace of God. The true self is the part of us that dares to be naked before the Creator and therefore finds its deepest desires met in the Divine.

The purpose of the spiritual disciplines is to help us stay in the true self, bring us into the presence of God. Often we hear the words 'spiritual disciplines' with the ears of the false self. We hear 'discipline', 'requirement', 'must' and 'should'. Instead, the spiritual disciplines are simply practices that help us to find God's love. You may simply sit in silence, letting God's love wash over you. You may walk quietly in a beautiful place and know the presence of the creator of that beauty. You may sing or dance as a loving response to the one who has given us song and movement.

As we learn to notice what helps us to stay in the true self, it is helpful also to be conscious of those things that draw us back into the false self. These may be requirements from without or needs from within. The requirements of our jobs or other responsibilities often make us feel as though we must put on the false self with its right way of doing things. We are aware of other people's expectations of us and so assume our old patterns of living up to expectations, whether real or imagined.

The inner needs may also drive us back to following our old scripts. A number of authors[13] suggest that Jesus' temptations[14] demonstrate to us the essential needs of human beings. Pennington[15] simply summarizes these as being what we do, what we have and what others think of us. Another way to look at them is to see them as the need for security, esteem and power and control.

First, Jesus is tempted to turn the stones into bread – to meet his own need for food and his very basic need for survival, safety and security – physical and psychological. For some people, this need for security is a core need that drives them back to behaving in 'proper' ways because then they feel secure, they feel as though the world will be a safe place. This reaction is often deeper than conscious thought, a well-entrenched script to which they default whenever they are threatened. A conscious choice must be made to trust that living with God is the safest way to live.

The second basic need is a need for esteem or approval. Many of us are constantly evaluating what others think of us and are addicted to trying to make them think well of what we do and are. Jesus' second temptation was to throw himself down from the pinnacle of the temple and let the angels catch him. This need 'to be spectacular', as Henri Nouwen[16] terms it, would certainly earn him the esteem of the people he came to win, even the esteem of the religious leaders.

Many of us have a deep need for esteem, for the approval of others, for others to think highly of us, and we will act out of the false self in all sorts of ways to gain their approval. Jesus did not give in to this shortcut way to gaining approval. Rather, he won the hearts of those around him by his integrity, his authenticity, his constant, unconditional love.

The third basic need, a basic human drive, is for power and control. This can be evidenced by a need to lord it over others, to be the one at the top, to tell others what to do. It may also be more subtly seen in the need to have things done 'the way I want them' or to have everything perfect. Jesus' third temptation was another shortcut to the kingdom, by gaining power. 'If you will bow down and worship me,' says Satan in the story, 'I will give you all the kingdoms of the world.'[17] Jesus could have rationalized that that, after all, was his life's purpose, but he recognized it as the way of power and control and he refused to let it trap him. The power of the kingdom is a much more subtle power – the power that wins the hearts of willing participants. Those of us who are looking for earthly power and control will often revert to the strategies of the false self to obtain them. We may even find that we use similar strategies to keep others in our power – appealing to their need for security, approval and control.

So we continue to dance across to the false self until, little by little, our scripts of the false self are replaced by the experience of God's love. Frequently there are core beliefs that drag us back to the false self, especially in times of crisis. That is when we need the spiritual practices and friends who will help us to focus on the God who delights in us and responds to our open hearts.

One of the outcomes of living in the arena of the false self is that we develop a sense of self-righteousness, entitlement, deserved reward. We have developed scripts for 'doing the right thing', for being right, for being good. Implicit in those scripts are that they will earn approval or other desired outcomes. In contrast, the outcome of living in the true self is a sense of freedom, of being loved for who we are and, therefore, joy and gratitude.

5

Gratitude and the true self

If living in the false self leads to shame or self-righteousness, living in the true self results in freedom and gratitude. This is the self that knows the rhythms of grace.[1] This is the self that can dance as a thankful response to life.

I was teaching in Myanmar (which is also called Burma) recently – one of the poorest countries in the world. At one point I was explaining the addiction cycle to some students. In Australia when I teach this we brainstorm a list of possible addictions – chocolate, alcohol, drugs, television, computer games, food, pornography, shopping and so on. We quickly make a long list. I realized when I did this in Myanmar that few of these things were available to these students. When they were unhappy or desperate, they prayed – there were not a lot of other options available. Despite their lack of these material things there was frequent laughter and a sense of contentment.

A survey was conducted exploring the happiness levels of people from different nations. It was not the western countries that were at the top of the list. Nations in the developing world were generally happier – the happiest being Nigeria. The researchers for the World Values Survey, 1991–2001,[2] described the desire for material goods as 'a happiness suppressant'. The West's riches and materialism have therefore come at a price. The price is contentment. We are not content with what we have. We are less likely to be happy, grateful and at peace than many in other poorer countries.

Early in Luke's Gospel there is a story of a woman who washed Jesus' feet with her tears.[3] This story often gets mixed up with the one about Mary of Bethany anointing Jesus' feet or the woman who anointed his head – an even bolder move. Both of those anointing stories are just before the Last Supper, but the story of washing his feet is earlier on. (It is unlikely that the woman was Mary Magdalene either – she is introduced in the following chapter.) It is a story of a 'woman who is a sinner', a woman of the streets who had an open heart. More open than those of the Pharisees who invited Jesus in. The Pharisees represent for us the false self because they think they know what they are entitled to, they believe they deserve a reward. In fact, they 'have their reward' in the form of the affirmation of men.[4] Today, our education and relative wealth have bred in us a sense that we are deserving, that somehow we deserve the riches we have, so we do not need to share them. We deserve the good jobs we have and the 'education we worked for' so that we can have that career. We have a sense of entitlement, even that the government should look after us.

In the Beatitudes chapter,[5] a little before the story of the 'sinful woman', Jesus is telling a different story. Blessed are the poor – in Matthew,[6] poor in spirit – for theirs is the kingdom of God. The kingdom of God is where God our King is present. Blessed are you poor, blessed are you when you know your need, for you will recognize God. Not like the Pharisees. Not like those of us who believe that we are deserving. It is easier for such people to not recognize God. Jesus said to the religious ones, 'You diligently study the Scriptures because you think that by them you possess eternal life. These are the Scriptures that testify about me, yet you refuse to come to me to have life.'[7]

The religious, self-righteous ones could not recognize Jesus, the one the scriptures testified to, because they were so sure that they had it all worked out and therefore deserved a God who rewards this kind of righteousness. The 'sinful' woman had no such blockages – her heart recognized the God who gives generously to the righteous and the unrighteous.

Joanna, let me tell you about this man I met. No, not like that! Don't laugh at me, it was something really different. You know this man people have been talking about? Some kind of teacher, goes round healing people? Well, I didn't see the healing stuff, but I was down at the markets and I saw people grouped around and he was there – just sitting, talking to people. I probably wouldn't have stayed – I don't have much time for God stuff usually – all about don't do this and don't do that and wash this and don't touch that. Me, I probably would never even get near the temple gates, but there was something different in the way that he talked about God. Like he was saying that it's not just about doing the right things or looking after people who look after you, but about loving your enemies and really caring for each other. I probably wouldn't have even stayed and listened to that – too high and mighty – except for the way he said it. Then, because he said, 'Then you will be children of the Most High, who is kind to the ungrateful and the selfish' and he called God our Father, saying, 'Be merciful even as your father is merciful' – not that I'd want God to be like my father, but I knew what he meant – I just started crying! Me! Usually I keep my feelings hidden really well, but if God really is like that – you know, merciful and kind – and it really isn't about keeping all those laws and rules and regulations . . . Anyway, I just couldn't stop crying. I ended up sitting near him while he chatted. He hardly even said anything to me and yet everything he said opened a whole new way of seeing the world. It made me feel like I could start my whole life again and nothing was held against me. There were a whole bunch of us there in the end, listening to him and asking questions.

Then some Pharisees came by. I heard them behind me, talking. It's a wonder they stayed, with all of us lot around. Of course, they were criticizing – something about the Sabbath and what you should and shouldn't do – but you could tell one or two of them were really curious, too. Then they decided that they should invite him to one of their places for dinner, get him on their own turf. No one really wanted him at their place, but they persuaded Simon. I know him because I'm friends with one of his kitchen staff. He's the kind of man who likes to please people, so he couldn't say no. So they invited Jesus over that night and Jesus said yes, he'd go. You can tell he's willing to give people a go. Well, I decided to go, too! I didn't ask them, but I knew that my friend would let me in – I could help in the kitchen. I was suspicious about these guys, too – what they'd say. I guess I just wanted to hear more of what this Jesus would say and if he'd say the same things to them – you know, like the stuff he had been saying to us – or change it, make it sound more like Pharisee talk. So I invited myself along! Yeah, I know, a bit cheeky, but Joanna, you have to understand, this man really got to me. I've met lots of men, you know that, but he's different. Listen, though, wait till you hear what happened.

I got a bit dressed up – after all, this was a Pharisee's house I was going to. I went early, got my friend to let me in and helped with the cooking and setting the tables, taking food in so that I had an excuse to go in there. Several of them were there a bit early, talking about what they'd ask him. They gave me a bit of a look when I came in to the room, like, 'Who's that tart Simon's got in?', but I didn't care – I had my excuse to hang around.

Then, when he arrived, they didn't really know how to treat him. They were rude. They didn't even have the servant wash his feet. I was annoyed with them, nearly said something, but then I saw his face – totally serene. You could tell that he wouldn't let the way they were get to him. I just started crying again – couldn't stop myself – and I didn't want to leave. Anyway, we'd done most of the work in the kitchen by then, so, when they all settled down on the couches, I sat down on the floor by his feet, just sat there with the tears running down my face. He didn't even stop me when the tears fell on his feet – he just looked at me with another of those looks, like, 'Everything's OK, you do what you have to do.' You know what? As I saw the splotches of tears on his feet – his dusty feet that they hadn't even bothered to wash for him – well, I decided that I'd wash them! That shows how much I was crying – it takes a lot of tears to wash someone's feet, but it was like all the tears of the last ten years were there, running down my face. Then I decided to go all out. I let down my hair and wiped them off. I hadn't been taking any notice of the other men, but I glanced up as I let my hair down. You should have seen the look, like, 'What are you going to do next, woman?' I think they thought that I was going to start taking my clothes off! They're such hypocrites. What do I care what they think. So, I started kissing his feet, too. Yeah, I know, it sounds over the top, but, look, you have to meet him. He makes you feel like you're a different person. All the muck that we put up with, it's not even there any more. I went and got some ointment, rubbed it into his feet. I mean, if you're going to do the job, do it properly, and all the time I was listening. He said all the same stuff to them, too – all the stuff about what God is really like.

Then, to top it off, you won't believe it, it was like he was show-ing that I am a better person than them! Me, better than the Pharisees! He said to Simon, 'I have something to say to you.' 'What is it, teacher?' said Simon, all nice. Well, he asked which person would be most grateful – the person who was let off of a debt of 50,000 or a debt of 1500. Pretty obvious, right. So Simon said, 'The one who was let off the most.' Walked right into Jesus' trap because then he turned to me and said, 'See this woman' – as if they might not have noticed me – and then he told them off about not washing his feet. You could tell, though, that it wasn't really about that. It was much deeper than that. He said, 'You didn't wash my feet, but she's washed them with her tears and wiped them with her hair. You didn't kiss me, but she hasn't stopped kissing me since I came in.' I hadn't either! I just kept wanting to touch him, thank him. 'You didn't anoint my head with oil, but she's anointed my feet with ointment.' I looked up then, looked Simon straight in the eye, like I was his equal. That's what I felt like. Then Jesus said the best thing of all: 'Therefore, I tell you, her sins, which are many, are forgiven, for she loved much.' I just keep saying it over and over to myself. Like this precious jewel I take out. 'My sins, which were many, are forgiven, for I love much.' I do, Joanna, I feel like I love the whole world, God, everyone. Maybe even the Pharisees! Not their God, though, this man's God – I love this God. Can you believe it? Me, talking about God like he's someone I know. Of course, the Pharisees didn't like it, started murmuring and that, like they do, looking down their noses. Jesus, though, looked straight at me and said, 'Your faith has saved you, go in peace', like it was something that I had done. My faith. You know what kind of faith I've had – faith that if you're nice to enough men at least you'll pay the rent and get to eat that week. If he means faith in the kind of God he's preaching, well, yes, I'm in. Who wouldn't be!

This woman understands grace in a way that the Pharisees could not grasp. She knew her need and so was open to other ways of being, new ways to God. Rainer Maria Rilke understands this neediness, the responsiveness of those who know themselves to be poor, thirsty:

> But you rejoice in the faces of those who thirst.
> You delight in all who cling to you for life.[8]

'You delight in all who cling to you for life.' When we know our neediness, then our hearts will open in response and gratitude. Meister Eckhart,[9] the fourteenth-century Christian mystic, said that if we have one prayer and it is a prayer of thanks, it is enough. A heart that is grateful is open and finds contentment. Feelings of entitlement can lead to a lack of gratitude if we do not get what we think we are entitled to. The outcome of this can also be self-pity, victimhood – a sense of injustice. The woman in the story has neither self-pity, nor a sense of entitlement, but a heart that is open and responsive. As a result, she is able to respond to a God of grace, a spirituality of grace – a God with whom she can dance.

6

Knowledge of good and evil

As someone who is aware of my need, I am able to recognize the good news of grace – of relating to a God who welcomes me simply as I am. Awareness of my true self, myself as one who cannot get to God by my own good deeds, helps me to see where the false self simply does not work. Contrasting the woman who washed Jesus' feet with the Pharisees, who did not, helps us gain an understanding of true self and false self and that can lead us into seeing law and grace with new eyes. Living in the place of a love relationship with our Creator God can be fairly easily understood as the place of the true self, the self that knows he or she is truly loved for nothing other than being. That it is God's grace, which brings life.

Recognizing that the false self is often the Pharisee part of us, which lives by the law, is a more subtle process. It is straightforward enough to think of the law as the standard that tells us what is right and wrong. We easily recognize that what the law is about is the identification of wrongdoing. Our response then is to turn away from wrongdoing and try to do better, to fulfil what the law requires. What Christians and religious people in general have not so easily seen is that the law has no power in and of itself to help us become righteous – all it does is hold up a mirror to show where we fall short.[1] So, we are caught on the treadmill of wrongdoing, repenting, trying to do better next time. Sometimes we succeed and sometimes we do not, but the law is not what gives us the power to succeed – it only holds up the standard against which we can evaluate ourselves.

The law seen as 'telling us what is wrong' is easy to understand. Another aspect of the law, however, which is often overlooked by Christians, is 'being good'. Most of us, as a result of our childhood upbringing, were taught to be good and so we learned the scripts of 'right behaviour'. How did we know we were good? The only way to know is to have some kind of comparison available. We have to have some kind of standard to measure ourselves by – some internalized script or external 'law'. We evaluate ourselves in relation to these and decide whether we have measured up or not. This process, however, is problematic. If we have failed, we are knocked back into Paul's lament – I do the things that I do not want to do and I do not do those things that I do want to do.[2] Who will deliver me? This is how we get on the treadmill of trying and failing. If, on the other hand we *have* measured up, we become caught up in the false self paradigm – the paradigm of self-righteousness and pride. Either way, the comparison process keeps us on the treadmill, where we measure ourselves against our internal scripts or external rules.

The only other way that we can measure whether we are good enough or not is to compare ourselves with others. This is even more problematic because we end up either condemning ourselves or these other people. The result of such comparisons, therefore, is self-righteousness or putdowns – of ourselves or others. We are still caught on the treadmill of not being good enough, which leads either to shame or thinking that we are better than others, leading, again, to condemnation of others and self-righteousness. This is the 'evaluation paradigm' – the paradigm of comparison, condemnation and shame.[3]

The evaluation paradigm is what the Garden of Eden story tells us is the 'tree of the knowledge of good and evil'.[4] Simply *knowing* of good and evil – having the law to measure ourselves against – is not the same as having the power to live in a way that we would like to. That was the trick of eating the fruit – we thought we could be 'as gods', we thought that knowing the law was enough to make ourselves righteous. We, as humans, thought that identifying what was right and wrong would enable us to be right, not be led into wrongdoing – things that harm ourselves or other people. Many societies, many individuals attempt this 'going it alone', which the tree of knowledge of good and evil represents – an attempt to do good without being in relationship with God.

The Garden of Eden story is telling us that doing good without spirituality, as independent beings without a God, is not how human beings were designed to operate. It is showing us that God's plan for human beings was not for us to lead an independent existence. God's plan was that we should eat of the tree of life – that is, live in a love relationship with him, walk hand in hand with our Creator God. If we do walk with God, in a life-giving relationship, we will fulfil the requirements of the law without even having to ask the question that the false self repeats over and over, 'Have I got it right? Am I good enough yet?'

The result, then, of living independently according to the law is being stuck on the treadmill of never being good enough – or, rather, being good just often enough to keep alive the illusion that we might be able to do it on our own. The reality is that we are, in fact, caught in the false self trap of trying endlessly to fulfil the requirements of the self and others, only to discover that condemnation or self-righteousness are the outcomes.

The belief that following the law, fulfilling requirements and doing the right thing, is the way to find the Divine is the trap of the false self, one that is deeply ingrained in the human psyche. What, then, is the way of the true self, the way into relationship with God, who does not evaluate, compare, condemn? What is the tree of life that the Creator has grown for us?

By coming to us in human form, God has given us a revelation of himself, of what this tree of life is. God has demonstrated his unconditional acceptance of us, his longing to walk in relationship with us. He has set us free from the strivings of the false self, bringing us into a love relationship with God.

One of the images that works for me, representing the true self in relationship with this God, is that of a parent with a toddler. I imagine a mother or a father whose little daughter is just beginning to take her first steps. I see the delight on their faces as they look at me, their little one, and see my small attempts. When I trip and fall, they do not scold me, as some of us fear that God would do – 'You stupid girl, stand

34

up, don't you know that humans walk on two legs, don't you dare fall over!' We can hardly imagine a loving parent speaking like that to their little one just learning to walk! No, instead the words would be, 'Up you get, little one, try again, you'll make it, you'll work it out. See, Mummy and Daddy are here to help you!' The father and mother would be hugely proud of their little one and delight in any small attempt she makes towards growing up.

For some of us, especially if we have been hurt in a parent–child relationship, that image may not work. It may be too difficult, as yet, to quiet the voice of the critical parent and believe that God is different. It may be that abuse has undermined the image of what a truly loving parent is like. Although such experiences are a powerful hindrance, many of us are able to relearn the positive kind of love when we become parents ourselves. When we recognize the mother heart or father heart in us, the heart that will do anything for this child, that revelation from our own inner lives can serve to change our core beliefs about how a loving parent, a loving God, sees us. If, however, that has not yet happened, a better image may be that of lovers.

Lovers see the best in each other, with total delight. It is not that they cannot see each other's faults, it is just that the faults don't matter, they can be overcome. Love accepts all. Love like that identifies with the beloved one and is always on-side, always willing to help the other overcome whatever he or she needs to. The true self understands that love. The true self is me when I know myself utterly loved just for who I am, one who can be a dance partner – not because I am such a good dancer, but because I place my hip against God's and follow his dance.

Even these pictures of human love fall short of the un-conditional love of our Creator God, the God incarnate in Jesus. They do, however, give us an indication of God's heart, how he feels about us, and what it might be like to live in the place of grace. They give us a window into what God planned when he made the tree of life for us to eat, when he created us in the Garden of Eden and walked with us in the cool of the evening.

Jesus also demonstrated this picture to us in the way that he lived in relationship with God. He did not keep telling his disciples to obey the law – rather, he modelled his love relationship with his father. He said that he does what he sees his Father doing.[5] 'I do nothing on my own but speak just what the Father has taught me.'[6] Jesus was showing us how to live in the new covenant. Rather than being ruled by an external law or set of rules, we are to turn to God, who lives within us. In the lifting up of our eyes to look into God's we find the way to live in a love relationship with God, which also brings good to those around us. Rather than being caught in a rule system, our own scripts, our society's norms and expectations or, as the Pharisees did, with a more and more intricate set of rules to govern each decision, we are simply to turn our eyes to the Divine, the one who lives within us.[7]

This might all sound too simple or too fraught with possible errors. The human Jesus, though, lived day after day in the spirit – in relationship with the one who loved him, showing us that we too can walk, as Paul put it, not under the law of sin and death, but in the spirit of life in Christ Jesus.[8] Jesus said that if we live in a love relationship with God and others, we will fulfil 'all the law and the prophets.'[9]

The creation story demonstrates simply but profoundly the difference between true self and false self, the difference between living under the law and walking in grace. God's long-term desire is that we live in a love relationship with him. This is eating of the tree of life and it was always God's plan that we should have life and have it abundantly. When we rejected this plan the first time, God found a way to restore us to life – through the crucifixion, Jesus' death on a tree.[10] A second tree of life came into being and our hearts could freely choose to walk in relationship with a God who died to bring us life.

The tree of knowledge of good and evil is a picture of the law – knowing in our heads what is right and wrong, having a standard by which to evaluate behaviour, but not necessarily having the power to live up to those standards. This was the serpent's temptation – 'you will be like God, knowing good and evil'[11] – but underlying it is a faulty worldview – the worldview that says humans are made to be autonomous beings, 'like God'. Instead, the Bible shows that we are made for relationship, that the self is not autonomous, as the West has come to believe, but, rather, is always a self in community.

Romans 7 is a powerful critique of the lie of becoming like God by eating of the tree of the knowledge of good and evil – the belief that we can autonomously obey the law. In verse 1 Paul says that he is writing to those who 'know the law'. Romans 7 and 8 are a comparison of the two ways of living – the first, trying autonomously to obey the law; the second, living in relationship with God: 'we serve in the new way of the Spirit [that is, in relationship with God in us], and not in the old way of the written code [that is, autonomously obeying the law] (Romans 7.6). Paul goes on to say what the old way was like: 'For what I want to do I do not do, but what I hate I do' (verse 15); 'I agree that the law is good' (verse 16) – that is, I know 'good and evil' and give mental, even heart-felt, assent to it, 'but I see another law at work in the members of my body . . . making me a prisoner of the law of sin' (verse 23) – that is, in my actual behaviour, I seem imprisoned, unable to do the very thing that I know is good. Paul's argument is that those who know the law, experience the impossibility of obeying it because they attempt to obey without the Spirit, without relationship with God. Romans 8 then contrasts strongly, saying that when we live 'according to the Spirit', in relationship with God, 'there is no condemnation' (verse 1), the requirements of the law are fully met in us (verse 4), we are children of God (verse 14) and heirs of God (verse 17).

The Romans 7 to 8 chapters, then, are not about sin having control over us as such. Rather, Paul is making the argument that the knowledge-of-good-and-evil way of living, the old covenant way – living as an autonomous being, trying to be righteous by obeying the law – just did not work. The only way to actually fulfil the law is to walk in relationship with God. When we live like this, we fulfil 'all the law and the prophets'.

The knowledge-of-good-and-evil paradigm is one of evaluation, condemnation and shame. It demonstrates to us that humans are, in that sense, set up for comparison and one-upmanship. If the only way that we can know that we are good enough is to compare ourselves with some standard or with each other, then we are caught in a paradigm of always comparing. Indeed, that is the way most of us live. From the moment we wake up we are evaluating – what kind of day is it, do we feel good, do we like what is on the agenda for the day, is breakfast how we like it? Every time we meet people, we are evaluating them, whether we like them, what kind of personality they have, what clothes they are wearing, how they react to us. Now, noticing difference is good, acknowledging what we like is a healthy process, but the destructive aspect of the evaluation paradigm is that we attach value and, therefore, too easily, condemnation – either to ourselves or others. His voice is too loud, (therefore I don't like him), her clothes are sophisticated (therefore I am not as good as she is), he speaks knowledgeably (so I am not as smart and therefore not as valuable as he is), she has an accent (therefore she is not one of us). The evaluation paradigm sets us up for condemnation and shame. This was not the original plan for the Garden of Eden.

Living in the false self, living by requirements, is to eat the fruit of the tree of knowledge of good and evil. Choosing a paradigm of evaluation, of knowing good and bad from a place of autonomy, has given us a mindset of constant evaluation. So it is that we continuously evaluate everything that happens around us, and within us, and find it wanting or else, perhaps, we are 'complacently pleased'[12] – an even worse place.

God's idea was that we should eat of the tree of life, walk in relationship with him and each other and experience life in all its abundance. When we walk in a love relationship with people, we are far less likely to be evaluating, criticizing and trying to change them or ourselves. Instead, we enjoy and we notice. Certainly we notice people's little foibles, but, instead of judging, we accept and appreciate the differences between them and ourselves. Living in a love relationship enables us to accept difference and imperfection and walk alongside other people, standing with them in their working out their salvation.[13]

The Garden of Eden story tells us nothing about being good. It tells us that Adam and Eve – humankind – were called to the dominion mandate (to look after the earth) to bring it to fruition. They were called into relationship with God and with each other. They tilled the garden, named the animals, walked with God in the cool of the evening and were one flesh with each other. There is no mention of rules and laws and certainly nothing about constant evaluation. The most specific comment about their relationships – with God and with each other – is that they were 'naked, and were not ashamed'[14] – a picture that is the antithesis of shame. The idea that they could be known, by God and each other, exactly as they were and know no shame is a wonderfully idealistic picture – and a glimpse of God's plan. That, indeed, is a picture of paradise on earth, with companionship, purpose and intimacy – all in the freedom of a shame-free knowing of each other and God. That is the essence of the gospel. We are called to freedom, to being real – not to being good. We are designed to live according to the true self – unashamed, in the arms of God – not the false self – all rules and seeking approval.

The Church was simply intended to be a community of believers – those who know themselves loved and can live together without shame. Traditionally, the Church has not been like this or, at least, not shown this face to the world. As a result, the one criticism that is levelled at the Church over and over is an accusation of hypocrisy. 'You hypocrites. You tell us to be good, but look at you.'

If the Church truly understood that it is not about evaluating and comparing and living up to standards, but, rather, being known for who we are in our relationships, being 'conspicuously imperfect',[15] but living in God's grace, then the world would be drawn to that reality and true humility. This is the paradise that we glimpse in the Garden of Eden, where Adam and Eve could be transparently seen for what they were and not be ashamed. That is what God calls us to – a place, a quality of our relationships with him and with each other in which we can be real and accepted anyway. That is the gospel in a nutshell. It's not about being good; it's about being real.

When Adam and Eve, and we in them, chose to eat of the fruit of the tree of knowledge of good and evil, we chose a righteousness based on comparison and living up to standards; a righteousness that had more to do with behaviour and doctrine than an attitude of the heart and relationship. We became caught in a mindset of comparison and evaluation that did not free us from wrongdoing but only showed us when we did wrong.

As a response to that choice, God gave us the law – a way of evaluating our behaviour that at least kept us in line with the way the world was designed. It was as though God said, 'You have chosen to live by a paradigm of evaluation, so let me at least give you some standards to evaluate actions by, some standards that fit with the way the world really is.' So, he told us not to steal from each other, not to commit adultery, not to kill, to worship only the God-who-is and to honour our parents 'that your days may be long.'[16] In other words, if you want to live well on this earth, then here are some basic rules to live by.

An exploration of the term 'law' might be helpful here. The law of gravity is a law that we are all very familiar with and constantly live by. It is not a law that commands us not to jump off a cliff, it is more that it explains to us what will happen if we do jump off a cliff. We cannot one day say, 'I don't think I will live by the law of gravity today.'

There is a series of cartoon drawings that illustrates this. A man with a sledgehammer is walking towards the stone on which the ten commandments are engraved. His intention is to break the law, to finally do away with it. One imagines the next picture to show the man with his sledgehammer and the stone tablets of the law in pieces. Instead, the law remains intact and the man ends up in pieces. So it is with the law of gravity. Jumping off a cliff results in the person being broken, not the law. However, there is a way for a person to jump off a cliff and remain intact, to fly even: if he jumps with the aid of a hang-glider or a parachute or a paraglider. As long as he obeys the laws of aerodynamics, he can 'break' the law of gravity. It is not that he is really breaking the law of gravity, of course – he is obeying a higher law that enables him to live more freely. So it is with the law of sin and death. As Paul explains in Romans 8, if we live by the spirit of life in Christ Jesus, we are set free from the law of sin and death. We no longer have to constantly evaluate our behaviour against a set of standards, because we live in a relationship that empowers us to fulfil the law and we do this by living in the law of love.

God gave us the law as a means of seeing ourselves as acceptable to him, only as a temporary measure. It was not God's original plan, nor was it his final response. The law was simply a way to bracket our behaviour until God could reveal a better way. The law was like a fence that kept us from wandering off into licence and perversion – like a schoolteacher, a babysitter, bringing us to God. As Paul puts it, 'So the law was put in charge to lead us to Christ . . . we are no longer under the supervision of the law.'[17] Paul is trying to explain that God's way was always a way of faith, was always about grace, but as a temporary measure, as we were living in the paradigm of evaluation, the law kept us in check, as a babysitter does, until the true relationship could be established once more.

Then, in Paul's wonderful words of freedom, God revealed a better way.

> When the time had fully come, God sent forth his Son, born of woman, born under the law, to redeem those who were under the law, so that we might receive adoption as sons. And because you are sons, God has sent the Spirit of his Son into our hearts, crying, 'Abba! Father!' So through God you are no longer a slave but a son, and if a son, then an heir.[18]

The old covenant, the law, resulted in slavery and condemnation. God's plan was, and is, that we should walk in life, in nakedness, in relationship with God, fulfilling all the law and the prophets in our love relationship with God, as God's children, and with each other, our brothers and sisters.

This walking with God in transparency, in nakedness, also means that, as I let others see me as I am, I learn to let them hold me in grace. A difficult lesson this one – to know it is my own judgements about myself that cause me to hold others at arm's length lest they see me too well. In holding others at arm's length, I hold myself back from receiving their embrace and the grace of the Father mediated through them. I prefer my image of my own self-righteousness and hold myself in isolation in order to retain it, but, slowly, as I receive the love of the Father, I can allow my defensiveness to thaw, little by little, and allow others to see the imperfect being that I am. It is only as I learn to hold the paradox of my own mix of light and darkness, that I can learn to celebrate with others their own patterns of shadow and light.

So, now we live under a new covenant, according to which righteousness is based on grace, not works. For many of us, this is a revelation that slowly unfolds. Indeed, Jesus' disciples do not seem to have truly understood the significance of what Jesus was about in this regard. The disciples, even though they lived with Jesus, understood that he was the Messiah, but did not seem to see things from the perspective of the new covenant. That was Paul's revelation.

7

Paul

———•◆•———

Paul's revelation of the new covenant – the new way to God –
is profound. I have set it down here by retelling Paul's story
as he has told us his life-story himself. Most of this chapter,
then, takes the form of direct quotes. My additions in between
aim to clarify the profound significance of the crucified Messiah,
which is that we have been released from living according to
law and the way of the false self. Paul understands more clearly
than any other biblical writer that the old covenant – the old
way of coming to God by fulfilling legal requirements – is
finished.

> Paul, an apostle – sent not from men nor by man, but by
> Jesus Christ and God the Father.[1] I am a Jew, born in Tarsus
> of Cilicia.[2] [I was] circumcised on the eighth day, of the people
> of Israel, of the tribe of Benjamin, a Hebrew of Hebrews[3] . . .
> brought up in [Jerusalem] at the feet of Gamaliel, educated
> according to the strict manner of the law of our fathers, being
> zealous for God . . .[4] My manner of life from my youth, spent
> from the beginning among my own nation and at Jerusalem . . .
> according to the strictest party of our religion I have lived as a
> Pharisee.[5] For you have heard of my former life in Judaism, how
> I persecuted the church of God violently and tried to destroy it;
> and I advanced in Judaism beyond many of my own age among
> my people, so extremely zealous was I for the traditions of my
> fathers.[6]
>
> I myself was convinced that I ought to do many things in oppos-
> ing the name of Jesus of Nazareth. And I did so in Jerusalem, I
> not only shut up many of the saints in prison by authority from
> the chief priests, but when they were put to death I cast my vote
> against them. And I punished them often in all the synagogues
> and tried to make them blaspheme; and in raging fury against
> them, I persecuted them even to foreign cities.[7]

Of course there were others who had claimed to be the Messiah. In fact my mentor, Gamaliel, generally advised that we should ignore such claims. An example of this was when the apostles were arrested in the very early days. What he said to the council was:

> Men of Israel, take care what you do with these men [the apostles]. For before these days Theudas arose, giving himself out to be somebody, and a number of men, about four hundred, joined him; but he was slain, and all who followed him were dispersed and came to nothing. After him Judas the Galilean arose in the days of the census and drew away some of the people after him; he also perished, and all who followed him were scattered. So in the present case I tell you, keep away from these men and let them alone; for if this plan or this undertaking is of men, it will fail; but if it is of God, you will not be able to overthrow them. You might even be found opposing God![8]

At first I followed his advice and simply ignored them. I began to get involved, though, when some of their followers were not following the Law. That's what the accusations were against Stephen, the first martyr:

> We have heard him speak blasphemous words against Moses and God.[9]
> This man never ceases to speak words against this holy place and the Law, for we have heard him say that this Jesus of Nazareth will destroy this place, and will change the customs which Moses delivered to us.[10]

Some said these were false witnesses, but I believed that anyone who brought obedience to the Law into question should be hunted down and killed. That's why I cast my vote with the stoning of Stephen, consenting to his death.[11]

When I realized what they were preaching about this Messiah, that totally convinced me that I needed to stamp out this new teaching. I'm not sure that they really understood what they were saying themselves. The first apostles were mostly uneducated, fishermen and so on. Peter's famous Pentecost preaching was mostly simply claiming that Jesus was the Messiah and that God had brought him back from the dead.[12] As Gamaliel said, if it wasn't from God, then it would all die out on its own, but then it came to my ears that they were preaching a 'crucified Messiah'. That changed everything for me. If this Jesus, their so-called Messiah, had been crucified, then he was cursed by the Law, because in our Law it is written:

Cursed is everyone who is hung on a tree.[13]

Being educated, knowing the detail of the Law as I do, I understood the significance of this better than they did. It seems for them, in those early days, they just thought of Jesus as the Messiah who healed and challenged us to a new way of living. They didn't realize the earth-shattering message that they were bringing. I saw it from a whole different perspective. If Jesus had been crucified – hung on a tree – then he was cursed by the Law, cursed by God, so he couldn't possibly have been sent by God. I knew that these two things were totally mutually exclusive. The very suggestion that someone crucified could be a Messiah made out that what the Law said didn't really count. That made me furious. As a Pharisee, I was ready to kill to defend the Law.

I persecuted this Way to the death, binding and delivering to prison both men and women, as the high priest and the whole council of elders bear me witness. From them I received letters to the brethren, and I journeyed to Damascus to take those also who were there and bring them in bonds to Jerusalem to be punished. As I made my journey and drew near to Damascus, about noon, a great light from heaven suddenly shone about me. And I fell to the ground and heard a voice saying to me, 'Saul, Saul, why do you persecute me?' And I answered, 'Who are you, Lord?' And he said to me 'I am Jesus of Nazareth whom you are persecuting.' Now those who were with me saw the light but did not hear the voice of the one who was speaking to me. And I said. 'What shall I do, Lord?' And the Lord said to me, 'Rise, and go into Damascus, and there you will be told all that is appointed for you to do.' And when I could not see because of the brightness of that light, I was led by the hand by those who were with me, and came into Damascus.[14]

My whole world was in upheaval.

For three days [I] was without sight, and neither ate nor drank.[15]

I had understood that a crucified Messiah was an impossibility. What I had believed was that preaching a crucified Messiah brought the Law into question. When I discovered that the crucified Messiah was a reality – I spoke to him on the road to Damascus – then I understood that, indeed, the Law was in question. Not that it now had no meaning for us, no, but, as the means to being accepted by God, the only way to live, yes, that covenant was finished. That, for a Pharisee, was disastrous – that's what I was thinking during those three days in Damascus, blind, fasting. I was going through, in my head, every bit of the Law. I was trying to imagine any other possible interpretation. There was no other meaning. If Jesus was the Messiah, then the Law, the old covenant, was obsolete.[16] That's what the scriptures had foretold, that God would establish a new covenant, a covenant that would change our hearts rather than be an external law.

> This is the covenant that I will make . . . I will put my law in their minds and write it on their hearts.[17]

Of course, I found out later that that's what Jesus himself had said when he told them to break bread and drink from the cup in memory of him. He said that it was the new covenant of his blood,[18] but the disciples didn't seem to have put all this together as I had. A Pharisee's mind thinks like that, sees the ramifications of such claims, and I spent three days sorting through these ramifications, receiving revelation of the gospel, of the significance of what Jesus had done.

> For I would have you know . . . that the gospel which was preached by me is not man's gospel. For I did not receive it from man, nor was I taught it, but it came through a revelation of Jesus Christ.[19]

It turned my world upside down. Once I understood it, the old Saul was dead. Everything had changed. We were no longer bound by the Law.

When some tried to bring the Law back in, I argued with them. When they tried to preach the gospel, but bring back just a part of the Law – circumcision – I said it could not be. It's all or nothing – grace or the Law.

> Again I declare to every man who lets himself be circumcised that he is required to obey the whole law.[20]

That's why I went to Jerusalem to lay before the apostles what I was preaching, when others came preaching a different gospel.

> Some men came down from Judea . . . and were teaching the brothers, 'Unless you are circumcised, according to the custom taught by Moses, you cannot be saved.'[21]

I went up by revelation; and I laid before them (but privately before those who were of repute) the gospel which I preach among the Gentiles, lest somehow I should be running or had run in vain. But even Titus, who was with me, was not compelled to be circumcised, though he was a Greek . . . [We did not yield to those who disagreed with] our freedom which we have in Christ Jesus, that they might bring us into bondage – to them we did not yield submission even for a moment, that the truth of the gospel might be preserved for you.[22]

That's why I disputed with them as I did. It cost me my whole life to understand that the Law now had a different meaning, to realize that the only way to God was grace. I was not going to let them water that down.

For he is not a real Jew [and, as Christians, we can add 'real Christian' here] who is one outwardly, nor is true circumcision something external and physical. He is a Jew who is one inwardly, and real circumcision is a matter of the heart, spiritual and not literal.[23]

[We] know that a man is not justified by works of the law but through faith in Jesus Christ . . . and not by works of the law, because by works of the law shall no one be justified . . . for if justification were through the law, then Christ died to no purpose.[24]

You have to understand, that is the core of being acceptable to God.

Then God said to Abraham, . . . 'My covenant . . . is to be . . . an everlasting covenant. Any uncircumcised male . . . has broken my covenant.[25]

If we agree that men do not have to be circumcised, we are changing the covenant, changing the way to God. It's not just about circumcision, it's about all the laws because they're about the covenant – the way we can come to God. We now come by grace alone. That's why I argued with Peter, too, about eating with the Gentiles.

When Peter came to Antioch, I opposed him to his face, because he was clearly in the wrong. . . . he used to eat with the Gentiles. But when they [some men from James] arrived, he began to draw back and separate himself.[26]

So, my dear brethren, understand what it means – that we no longer live under the old way of coming to God. The Law was a temporary measure:

> our custodian, until Christ came.[27]
> For all who rely on works of the law are under a curse; for it is written, 'Cursed be everyone who does not abide by all things written in the book of the law and do them' . . . if a law had been given which could make alive, then righteousness would indeed be by the law.[28]
> If you are led by the Spirit you are not under law.[29]

My beloved children, *that* is the good news. We are no longer in the bondage of the Law, having to get everything right according to religious rules and regulations. We are in a direct relationship with the God of grace.

> It is for freedom that Christ has set us free. Stand firm, then, and do not let yourselves be burdened again by a yoke of slavery.[30]

Many of my letters come back to this understanding because so many have failed to understand it. So many Christians have not really taken hold of this new covenant. The new covenant is really the original one. God's original design, revealed in Christ, is that we can come to God by grace. Indeed, that the only way to God is grace – a response of faith to a God of love.

8

The crucified Messiah – a God of descent

———•◦•———

Paul tells us over and over that the gospel he preaches is one of grace. In other words, we are not to live a religion of self-righteous law-keeping, but can come to the crucified Messiah only by becoming like him. How is it, then, that our theology since has lined us up more with the Pharisees than with the tax collectors?

Many of us have received a religion that mixes together the Messiah as a king, coming in triumph, and the crucified one, the Christ of the Cross, the God of the hymn in Philippians, who: 'though he was in the form of God, did not count equality with God a thing to be grasped, but emptied himself [made himself of no reputation], taking the form of a servant, being born in the likeness of men. And being found in human form he humbled himself and became obedient unto death, even the death on a cross.'[1]

We have done just what the first disciples did and looked for a king who would free us from our oppressors by means of power. We have misunderstood the nature of the dance – thinking that a king would come and force everyone to do things his way. A dance of humility and love and reciprocity is an entirely different matter. There are several instances when the disciples demonstrate their expectation of just such a 'power dance' – using power to correct others, rather than the way of descent. With the third temptation in the desert, Jesus faced this choice – the possibility of taking power, receiving 'the kingdoms of the world' in a way other than the way of descent, the way of the cross, and he refused it. The same temptation, in a different form, was put in front of him again

49

when he was trying to explain to the disciples that he must go to Jerusalem to die and Peter tried to dissuade him from doing so. Having just confessed Jesus as the Messiah, Peter had no conception that his was the way of descent, not ascent.[2] He expected ascent to power, not descent to death.

There are several other instances of the disciples' reactions that show an expectation that the kingdom is about power, rather than descent. The arguments over who is the greatest[3], who will sit at Jesus' side in the kingdom[4] and even whether or not they could call fire down from heaven on a village that did not receive them,[5] all, in essence, spring from this view. Very early in Jesus' ministry, the disciples were involved in healing and miracles, but right up until the last supper, they still had not grasped the way of descent[6] that Jesus was trying to explain to them.

In these events, the human need for power and control are demonstrated. The Church, over the centuries, has frequently demonstrated a similar lack of understanding of Jesus' message – using power, domination, control and outright war to maintain itself. Over and over, men and women, such as Francis of Assisi and Teresa of Calcutta, have tried to call the Church back to the way of descent.

Whereas the focus of much of the western world is on ascent, to success and status and power, the way of being that Christ shows us is that of descent, to take the form of a servant, to humble oneself, even to accepting death. Gordon Cosby, who founded ministries for the destitute and homeless in a poor area of Washington that is walking distance from the White House, explains that this God, the God of the Gospels and Paul's letters, is a 'descending God': 'In the Gospels it is quite obvious that Jesus chose the descending way. He chose it not once but over and over again. At each critical moment he deliberately sought the way downward.'[7] Again, 'it becomes plain to us that God has willed to show his love for the world by descending more and more deeply into human frailty . . . God is the descending God. The movement is down, down, down, until it finds the sickest, the most afflicted, the most helpless, the most alienated, the most cut off. The truest symbols that we have of Jesus are the lamb – the lamb led to the slaughter, a sheep before its shearers being dumb. Total poverty: a dumb sheep, the Lamb of God, and the Servant Christ kneeling with a towel and a basin, washing feet on the eve of his crucifixion. The weeping Christ riding into Jerusalem on a donkey.'[8]

Many Christians have somehow perceived that, because we are on this side of the resurrection, our gospel has become one of triumph and have thought that that means we come in power rather than descent and humility. We now identify with the Lion of Judah rather then the lamb. It is not the Lion of Judah coming in dominant power who is worthy to open the scroll that ushers in the end of time, though, but the lamb. The apostle John recounts his vision: 'I wept and wept because no one was found who was worthy to open the scroll . . . Then one of the elders said to me "Do not weep! See the Lion of the tribe of Judah . . . is able to open the scroll. Then I saw a Lamb, looking as if it had been slain, standing in the centre of the throne." '[9] It was by being the Lamb that Jesus conquered death and it was by dying that he defeated the powers and authorities, 'triumphing over them by the cross.'[10] Cosby notes that it was his death that turned our hearts to him also: 'What was it that captured our hearts? It was that figure dying on a cross . . . If the Lamb of God . . . the form of the Servant Christ giving his life away for others – for me – if those deep expressions of reality captured my spirit, literally broke my hard heart of stone and gave me a heart of flesh, ended my captivity and delivered my spirit, why do I think that the expression of authority or power or success or efficiency is going to break anybody's heart?'[11]

This descending God shows us the way of *kenosis*, of self-emptying. Maggie Ross in *Pillars of Flame*, explains that this is what our faith is about: 'The heart of Christianity is the self-emptying, kenotic humility of God expressed in Jesus the Christ . . . At the heart of God's humility is this: God willingly is wounded.'[12] He is 'a kenotic living God who is unceasingly self-outpouring, compassionate, and engaged with the creation . . . God's inviolable vulnerability, God's unswerving commitment to suffer with and within the creation, to go to the heart of pain, to generate new life, hope, and joy out of the cry of dereliction, out of the pain to utter self-denudation, utter self-emptying, utter engaging love.'[13] This is the God Jesus came to tell us about and to show us – the willingness to give, suffer the pain of loss and wounding, hold back in patient waiting, respond in self-forgetting joy and forgiveness.

The spirituality of descent is the practice of a spirituality that knows this descending God. Rather than the all-powerful Zeus, god of the Greeks, prodigal children know the God who gives, the God who waits, the God who experiences the shame and brokenness of his own children. This descending God seeks to serve, not to be served, not just in Jesus' lifetime but in the millennia following, including in the present world where it is so easy to choose ascent, success, status, positions of power in our churches and 'Christian' institutions. Jesus deliberately broke the religious rules – the purity codes[14] – of his culture in order to include the outcasts. Time after time, at meals, in the homes of Pharisees, in public places, he knowingly touched the untouchables – the bleeding woman, the leper, the Samaritan woman and others the 'rules' forbade him to touch. We need to think about this as 'Suppose the only God that exists is the descending God. Suppose the only way we can know God is to go down, to go to the bottom . . . If God is going down and we are going up, it is obvious that we are going in different directions. And we will not know him. We will be evading God and missing the whole purpose of our existence.'[15]

The descending God, then, is one who serves, one who lets go of position and status and power in order to touch the lives of those around him: 'We have seen what Jesus was like. If we wish now to treat him as our God, we would have to conclude that our God does not want to be served by us, he wants to serve.'[16]

It is important to notice that Jesus' descending is not a 'doormat' kind of servanthood. He is not trapped, as many of us are, in serving because he wants others to see how good he is, how humble he is. It is a servanthood that comes from knowing that he is accepted by God, not a serving in order to gain that acceptance. John makes this clear at the beginning of the story of the Servant Christ who washed his disciples' feet: 'Jesus, knowing that the Father had given all things into his hands, and that he had come from God and was going to God . . . girded himself with a towel.'[17] Jesus was a servant who also knew his

identity. He was not serving as one who did not know his boundaries or one trying to earn approval – he knew who he was –
but knowingly chose to serve, knowingly chose the lower place,
knowingly went to the cross, the final point of nakedness and
brokenness. There he displayed for all time the character of the
Creator God – in Ross' phrase, 'God's inviolable vulnerability'.

As we reflect on this God, the crucified one, the prodigal father
who stoops to embrace the sinner, we know that Jesus is indeed
God's self-disclosure: 'the cosmos is ruled by a self-giving Love
who chooses to endure crucifixion rather than decree any abridg-
ment of human freedom.'[18] God is so committed to allowing
us the freedom of our own choices that, in Jesus, he refuses to
call down fire from heaven against those who disagree with him,
he refuses to call down legions of angels to stop those taking
him to death: 'We cannot have it both ways. We cannot have
a God who is an iron-handed ruler in remote control of the
cosmos and, at the same time, a historic incarnation of that God
who consistently defines himself as a servant . . . [We must]
choose between a God enthroned in the power of imperial
privilege and a God "disenthroned" in the more exquisite power
of servanthood.'[19]

The paradox is that, once we have glimpsed this servant king
who tells us that his flesh must be our real food, we must learn
to feed on his brokenness and self-giving so that, even though
we may be tempted to shrink back, we are so drawn to him that
we say, as Peter did, 'Lord, to whom shall we go? You have the
words of eternal life.'[20] Even then, we may, as Peter did, be pre-
pared to give our lives to fight for him, but yet not know how
to give ourselves to the way of surrender and powerlessness that
the Lamb shows us. This, though, is the way to life: 'Just as
crucifixion and resurrection form the centrepiece of the life and
work of Jesus, so too the cross and its promise of life reborn are
central to his invitation to live.'[21] The crucifixion is not just a
plan God thought up to 'fix things' after we humans rebelled:
'The Crucified God is simply the eruption into history of the
cosmic redemptive love that is built into the structure of the
universe from its start. The book of Revelation speaks of Jesus
as "the Lamb slain from the foundation of the world." '[22] It is
in coming to know this God that we can come to acknowledge

the deepest, most broken places of ourselves and bring them into the light of his life-giving grace.

This is a God who allows himself to die, even protects his death, setting his face like flint towards Jerusalem, and even allows an unbelieving world to watch as he wrestles with isolation and abandonment. This is a God who can cry out at his death the truth of his reality, 'My God, my God, why have you forsaken me?'[23] Why even the revolutionaries and atheists, says Chesterton, could identify with *this* God.

> And now let the revolutionists of this age choose a creed from all the creeds and a god from all the gods of the world, carefully weighing all the gods of inevitable recurrence and of unalterable power. They will not find another god who has himself been in revolt. Nay (the matter grows too difficult for human speech), but let the atheists themselves choose a god. They will find only one divinity who ever uttered their isolation; only one religion in which God seemed for an instant to be an atheist.[24]

Chesterton recognized that God himself has been as we are and so has shown the way to a spirituality that is honest and naked in a world that is broken, so we can live with the truth of who we are, even at our worst. This, then, is true relationship with God – a faith that God is present; even though the floods may come and the fire, God is present. This relationship enables us to journey with others in their wilderness and darkness, having faith that God, is for them and with them, too: 'Faith is not assent to doctrines or surrounding ourselves with props and propositions. It is trust that God – as Christ shows us – has been there before us, goes within us, waits to find us beyond the edges of utter dark. And, found by God, we become aware that God is closer to our being than we are.'[25]

God has lived through life, death and life, has shown us the way through and now is present within each of us as we walk our journeys, enabling us to go to the places of brokenness and death within ourselves because God is a God of descent.

9

Learning the path of descent – Peter's story

━━━◆•◆•◆━━━

What does it mean in terms of everyday life to live the way of descent? The disciples learned this only very slowly. Not until the revelation of Jesus' death did they understand it. Peter, wanting to follow Jesus into everything, certainly had not learned it, even at the last supper. Only through his recognition of what it meant for Jesus to go down to the lowest place, and of his own unwillingness to go there, did he begin to understand that way of living.

As I read Peter's story, I notice my own struggle with accepting my weaknesses. I see how easily I choose the way of ascent, the way of trying to prove that I am better than I really am. I notice how much mental energy I waste defending my actions to myself and comparing myself to others. I see how riddled is my thought life with comparison and competition, even though I thought that I knew about the uselessness of the paradigm of evaluation. I thought that I had learned how to live according to the true self, accepting myself and others, but so often I find myself, especially when I am under pressure, comparing, proving my own superiority. I am just better than Peter at keeping it hidden.

Maybe it helped Peter to know himself, being such an extrovert. So many times he had blurted things out without thinking. So many times he had been corrected publicly for his foolishness or unkindness. I am grateful to him for his blurting – he says what so many of us keep hidden in our heads. Many times I have been glad that I am an introvert and haven't exposed what I would like to have said. My introversion has allowed me to keep my mask of niceness, my façade of kindness. Only gradually have

I been able to admit that I am as judgemental as everyone else, as foolish as Peter and as arrogant and self-serving as the rest of the human race. Peter was exposed often, so could learn in leaps and bounds. I admire his courage in letting himself be seen and am envious of how much he grew as a result.

I imagine myself observing some of this learning in the every-day event of walking with Jesus, like the time Peter and the other disciples were arguing about who was the greatest. This on the eve of Jesus facing the supreme test of humility and self-giving. Luke places it right in the context of the last supper.[1] On another occasion it was when they were out walking.[2] I picture myself present with them.

> Today, as we were out walking, I was listening to the men as usual. They were talking about themselves, comparing them-selves, and then, finally, arguing about who was the best, who was greatest. In my heart I was judging them, but actually join-ing in: 'I'm more spiritual than that; oh you've misinterpreted that piece of scripture – I know the scriptures better than you, known them since I was a child; how little you understand people; you don't even get the spirituality of descent that Jesus is trying to show us' and on and on.
>
> So, when Jesus asked them, 'What were you talking about on the way?' I was so glad I hadn't joined in. I rather enjoyed seeing them squirming. Then he turned and looked at me. Those eyes – so penetrating, yet loving, all at once. I squirmed, too. The little hint of a question at the edge of his smile said, 'You too?' I could only answer with my eyes, 'Yes, me, too. Oh change my heart.'
>
> Then Jesus took a child and said, 'Whoever receives one such child in my name . . . receives him who sent me.' Now what was that about? He'd already said we were to become as children, but to receive a child? What does he mean to receive a child? I guess you don't judge children, you don't compare yourself with children. Is opening my heart to a child how to open my heart to receive the mystery of God?

Peter was shown up publicly a number of times, but was able to respond in such a way that eventually he became a leader in the early Church, with his weaknesses known to all. I think that his journey to self-forgiveness was aided by the encounter with Jesus over breakfast one day. Richard Rohr[3] says that the reason we know it is a safe universe is that God-become-man does not mete out any form of recrimination for the disciples running away from the Garden of Gethsemane. Not a word is said to anyone in accusation. Surely if we had been Jesus we would have let out a few 'I told you so's or let them know of our hurt and anger. The closest he got was this story of reinstating Peter – of letting Peter know that he is understood and forgiven.[4]

Peter allows the stories of his many mistakes, including his denials, to be told everywhere. There are not many stories that appear in all four Gospel accounts – not even Jesus' birth is told in all of them – but that of Peter's denials is in each one. Whenever it was that the Gospels were actually written down, the presence of this story in each one suggests that it had become an integral part of the story of the crucifixion. What must it have been like for Peter to have that story told and retold wherever the Gospels went? It remains a profound story of human weakness and lack of self-knowledge.

I have tried to imagine what it must have been like to try and grasp the reality of what Jesus was saying for the men and women who lived with him. Peter makes it clear in his letters that he knew what it was like to live in Jesus' life-changing presence: 'We did not follow cleverly invented stories when we told you about the power and coming of our Lord Jesus Christ, but we were eyewitnesses of his majesty.'[5]

Eyewitnesses to what he was truly like, to what God is truly like, we lived with him day after day – through praise and honour and through criticism, even torture. He explained many things to us, even when we were slow to understand, slow to respond – even, in the end, when we turned against him and then when we feared him gone for ever. Let me tell you of the profound learning of those last days.

I had wanted to follow him every step of the way. I had declared in front of everyone that that is what I would do, that I would die for him if need be. He had gently explained to me that I would not be able to. I remember, though, the conviction I had that I would. I'd even borrowed a sword from a friend so I had something to defend us with. I was determined that I would fight if need be and I did. You have heard the accounts of the high priest's steward and how I cut his ear off. Admittedly not a death-dealing blow, but I'm not a practised swordsman after all. The point I am making is that I did get in there and start to fight, start to defend Jesus, as I had declared that I would, but then Jesus turned the tables on me, on my understanding, as he had so many times before. 'Put away your sword,' he said. He made it clear that it was not the time to fight, told them who he was and that they were to let us go. Then he let himself be led away by them. I was totally taken by surprise. In retrospect I saw that this is what he had been trying to tell us, but back then I simply could not understand him, could not understand his reasoning, did not understand the logic of his self-giving. As far as I was concerned, these were the enemy, the ones he had been arguing with, clashing with more and more strongly. It didn't surprise me that it had finally come to this, to carrying a sword, fighting, threats of death. What I was unable to understand, though, was that the higher way was to go with the enemy, to allow the earthly powers to take him and trust God with the outcome. I just did not know what was going on. All I could do was stay nearby. I was determined to at least keep that part of my promise to him.

I followed along behind the soldiers taking Jesus away. I was shocked by it all, though. I was so confused and terrified for my life. As I said, I had already faced the possibility of dying, of fighting for our lives, but I had imagined myself shoulder to shoulder with Jesus, defending the truth of what he was teaching, the truth of who I had come to know him to be. They took him to the high priest's house. I could see John ahead of me and he just went on in with the soldiers. I remembered that he knew the high priest so no one questioned him being there, but I got to the gate and had no reason to give for my wanting to go in. I just stood there, afraid to ask to enter, afraid to identify myself now that everything had got out of control, but not wanting to let myself turn and run either. Then John came and spoke to the girl on duty at the gate and got her to let me in. 'You are not one of his disciples, are you?' she said to me, and in my fear I said no, not daring to be known among these people. John tried to edge up as close as he could to find out what was happening, but I hung back, hearing only bits and pieces of what was going on. I still just had no understanding of what Jesus was on about. This giving of himself to the enemy, the standing in silence as they accused him and brought all sorts of rabble against him – I just had no idea how I was supposed to respond. I felt as though

the last three years were being hacked to pieces in front of me –
all that we had been through together being taken away from us
for nothing.

The night was cold and some of the servants were standing
around a fire in the courtyard to keep warm. I went and
stood with them and listened to the talk, not knowing what
else to do. The girl from the gateway came by and saw me there.
She said to the others, 'He was with this Jesus, the Nazarene'
and one of the men looked at me and said, 'Yes, you're a
Galilean, too.' Again I denied it – what else could I do? I was
afraid they'd take me to the chief priest as well, then and there,
and I had lost all my bearings, all my sense of where Jesus was
heading in all of this.

I stepped back, out of the circle, tried to find John, then went
and stood in the shadow of the entryway where no one would
be able to see me. I'll admit it. Part of me just wanted to cut and
run, leave it all behind, get out of Jerusalem as fast as I could
and get back to my family, to the life that I had had before Jesus
ever appeared. However, I had sworn to Jesus and to the
others that I, of any of them, would stay with him. John was in
there somewhere and if he could stay, then I could, too.

I stood there in the cold and the dark shadow, trying to make
up stories as to why I was there and think how we could get
Jesus out of it. Of course I just came up against a brick wall
every time. Jesus had given himself to them and, from what
I could piece together of what was going on, he was refusing
to defend himself.

During this time I was trying to find a way to make sense
of what was happening, but it never occurred to me what I had
done – that I had already denied him as he had said I would. I
was too busy defending myself in my own mind, too busy trying
to understand it all.

Different people came and went round the fire and I wanted
to find out what was going on. The girl who had been at the
gate had gone and, as the night wore on, I decided to go and
warm myself again. I could maybe catch a glimpse of what was
happening to Jesus from there, too, so I slipped in among the
servants and tried to join in the conversation. Then one of the
men heard me talking, turned, looked me full in the face and said,
'Didn't I see you with him in the olive grove?' Of course I denied
it again, swore that I didn't know what he was talking about, that
I didn't even know Jesus.

In the silence that followed my outburst, I heard a cock crowing and I remembered what Jesus had said: 'Before the rooster crows twice you yourself will disown me three times.' In horror, I turned towards where they held Jesus and there he was, turned towards me. I could hardly take it in. In the centre of the maelstrom of accusation and counteraccusation was this stillness. I knew that they had already beaten him, mocked him and were likely to soon drag him off to his death and, somehow, in the middle of all that, he had heard the cock crow and turned to look for me.

This you may hardly believe. It was almost as though there was no one else around. He looked down into the courtyard, and met my eyes. There was no condemnation, no 'I told you so', just a look of deep compassion, compassion for a friend in need, as though he was trying to communicate to me, 'Peter, I told you that you would not be able to stand with me. I knew you had not understood. That's why I told you, so that when it happened you would not lose heart.'

I couldn't handle it. I turned and stumbled out of the courtyard, found a corner of the dark empty street away from the fire and the lights and wept bitterly. Bitter self-recognition, bitter acknowledgement that I am what I am, I did not have the courage I thought I had, I was not ready to follow Jesus everywhere as I thought I could and I was not ready to be a leader in this kingdom of his, as I had been so sure before that I could be.

Later, we found out what had happened to Judas, how he had received money from the chief priests to betray Jesus. You can imagine how angry we were, but then I thought of what I had done and knew I was no better than Judas — I too had betrayed Jesus, just in a less direct way. Then we found out that Judas had tried to give the money back. I could imagine his own bitter self-recognition and, I have to say, I sympathized with him. The difference between us was that Judas was unable to forgive himself and went and hung himself. He could not face himself and what he had done. Maybe that was the difference between us. I had made so many public mistakes, been rebuked by Jesus so many times already and maybe knew my own weaknesses a little more than Judas so that, when I was faced with the reality of my weakness, I wept bitterly, but at least I didn't kill myself. I had that look to hold on to — that look from Jesus showing his understanding and forgiveness. Still,

I couldn't face him. I didn't go and see him die on the cross. We left that to the women and John. Somehow they had a different kind of courage. Mine, I can see now, was full of bluster and self-importance.

So, I only heard about his death second-hand, when I finally gathered back with the others on the Sabbath, the day after they had killed him. We shared together everything we knew, pieced together the story. I told them, in tears again, of what I had done, that I had betrayed him at the last, no better than anyone else. They understood – I guess they know me better in some ways than I know myself. They know how human I am and that I am having to accept my weaknesses, my shortcomings, and that Jesus knows them, too.

Something happened that really transformed the way that I thought about all this. It changed me from someone who doubted myself and my place in the kingdom that Jesus had tried to explain to us. We had decided to go out fishing – well, I had decided, really. I couldn't work out what we were supposed to be doing, so I went back to what I had known before we had ever heard of Jesus. We were back up in Galilee and I was a bit tired of the mystery of it all, so I said to the others, 'I'm going fishing. Come with me if you want to.'

A bunch of us went out fishing all night – caught nothing. As it was getting light, we saw someone on the beach. He called out to us, asking if we had caught anything. When we said that we hadn't, he directed us to another spot and told us where to cast the nets. Well, they came up full of fish. John looked again at the man on the beach and told me that it must be Jesus. I didn't want to wait a moment longer, impetuous as I still am, so I jumped overboard, leaving the others to pull in the nets. It was Jesus all right, cooking some fish over a fire and looking as serene as ever.

After we had hauled all the fish in and breakfasted, he drew me aside. I was expecting a rebuke – as yet he had said nothing about my betrayal and I knew that he knew what had happened. Instead, he asked me if I loved him more than everything else.[6] I couldn't answer him – not the way he asked it because I knew that the implication was whether I would do anything for him, follow him anywhere. Before his death, before my betrayal, I would have said yes, would have claimed sacrificial dying if need be, but now I knew myself better. All I could answer was that I was his friend, that he knew I loved him,[7] but he

61

didn't rebuke me. Instead, he just said, 'Feed my lambs.' However, then he asked me again, using the same words, 'Peter, do you love me, love me unreservedly?' Again, I knew that I couldn't say yes. 'Jesus, you know I am your friend,' I said. 'Take care of my sheep,' he said. Then he asked a third time if I loved him. This time he said it differently, used the words I had used: 'Simon, son of John, are you my friend?' I was hurt that he asked me again when I had tried to say as honestly as I could all that I was able to say.

It was only afterwards, talking to John, that I realized the significance of what he had done. He had asked me first if I would sacrifice everything and I had had to answer with the new self-knowledge that I was his friend. The third time he used my words, so came to me where I was, asked me only if I could do the little that I knew I could. He was letting me know that what I could do was enough. 'Feed my sheep,' he said.

I realized something else, too. When he had looked at me there in the high priest's courtyard, I had just denied him three times and we both knew that I had done it. Now he was giving me the chance to say three times that I loved him, as honestly as I was able to do. No hint of recrimination, just a reinstatement – a recognition that I am a valued disciple, one who will look after the believers – the sheep without a shepherd – whom he had come for. Then, in case there should be any doubt in my mind, any tendency to give it all up and go back to fishing, he looked at me deeply and said, 'Follow me', only this time I knew that he meant follow him to death, follow him in a self-giving life, to whatever end it brought me. A great joy welled up in me. I knew that he knows me through and through, knows my weaknesses, accepts them, but still trusts me to walk in his footsteps, has confidence in all of us that we will walk with God ourselves, relies on us for the furtherance of the kingdom.

As Peter faced the reality of his humanness with Jesus, as well as his need, therefore, to walk with God, he was free to live out of the best in himself. He was not caught, like Judas, in death-dealing self-accusation. Daniel Ladinsky draws on Persian mystic Jalal ad-Din Muhammad Rumi, when responding to the question of our human tendency to torture ourselves with our past or fears for the future:

Why lay yourself on the torturer's rack of the past and
future?
. . . Be kind to yourself, dear – to our innocent follies.
Forget any sounds or touch you knew that did not help
you dance.[8]

I have come to realize that one of the reasons I lay myself
on the torturer's rack of the past is that I want to be better
than I am and I want people to think well of me – really,
to think that I am better than I actually am. My gyrations of
replaying old events is not dancing but the torturer's rack – I
am trying to prove to myself that I am better than I am. I am
learning instead to say, 'This is part of being human. I make
mistakes. I am human.' Peter's weaknesses and mistakes – his
humanness – are known to the world. My unwillingness to
make mistakes proves my unwillingness to be part of humanity.
Instead, it is a desire to put myself in God's place, a desire for
ascent.

Slowly, as I am willing to face my weaknesses and my
mistakes, comparisons and need for approval, I find the God
who is already at the lowest place. The more I am willing
to admit about the false self, the more I see the beauty of my
true self. Slowly I can respond to God as a child, one who does
not need to deserve anything, but just is, loved for who I am
and nothing else. I trust that the words 'You are my beloved
child, in whom I am well pleased'[9] also apply to me simply
because I am and my desire is from and towards God.

My own struggle to be good enough and so 'deserve' God's
approval, as though I need to be 'deserving' for God to work
through me, is a long, slow journey. There are some who are
more easily able to believe that deserving is not the right way
to understand our relationship with God, and with ourselves.
Mary is such an example. She accepted God's favour, but not
because she thought that she deserved it. No, rather, because
she understood that this is what God is like – one who comes
to the least, the undeserving, the little ones. This, too, is the way
of descent – the acceptance of God's love, God's 'favour', without even asking whether we deserve it or not.

10

Mary's story

An angel visited me the other day.

Imagine it! Imagine saying that to anyone! An angel came and talked to me. Who can I even talk to about this?! An angel came and sat down and talked to me. Truly, that's what happened.

I was sitting out by the stream, down below the town. I had gone to gather some flowers for the dinner table because we have guests coming. My mother knows how I love to decorate the table with flowers, so, after we had done the basic preparations, she shooed me out. 'OK Mary, off you go – I know that you want to go outside and find some flowers. I can get on with the rest of it now you've helped.'

So off I went, down the hill to the stream where I love to go, where the little lilies grow sometimes in the shade. Often I will just stay there for a while and look out over the valley. If I sit very quietly, the birds come and hop around or sit up high in the tree and sing. Sometimes I lie on my back and watch the clouds and I imagine all sorts of things in their shapes. That day I lay there, too, looking up into the sky. I didn't want to pick the flowers too quickly and have them wilt while I was day-dreaming. I lay on my back and thought about all sorts of things. About the birds and their lives, in the midst of this beauty all the time. About how the little swallow chicks I'd seen under the rafters of the synagogue squawked so loudly the minute the mother bird appeared. They open their mouths so wide and carry on as though they are starving and she's forgotten them. As if she would. I smiled as I thought of their demands, not for a moment caring that then everyone knew where they were. The chicks were totally trusting that they were safe and that their parents would respond to them, as long as they chirped loudly enough.

I thought about the lambs I passed running back to their mothers every now and then as the mothers cropped the grass or rested in the shade. I thought about the sound of the stream as it chattered its way over the rocks. I daydreamed a little about what life will be like when I'm married, when I'm a mother with little children and how I'd like to show them all of this – the anemones that peep out from under the tussocks of grass, the catkins growing among the spring leaves, the soft down floating from them. I thought about God and how he had made all of this beauty. I noticed the warmth of the sun on my skin and imagined it as his love pouring out of the sky. Then, suddenly, there was an angel.

I know, it sounds like it was part of my daydreaming, but it wasn't. Really, in some ways it was very ordinary. No wings. No flying down out of the sky. Just a person sitting there on the grass beside me. I'd been lying with my eyes shut, so my first thought was that I'd been so away in my own world that I hadn't heard him come up. Now, that's a funny thing. I thought the angel was a him. It's usually men I see when I'm out walking – the shepherd boys or men walking to the next village – so, when I see someone in the distance, I expect it to be a man. Afterwards, though, when I was thinking about it, I realized that I didn't know. The clearest memory is how wonderful he felt to be near – just peaceful and calm . . . and somehow beautiful. It's hard to describe, really. It was more about what I felt being with him than what he looked like.

So, as I opened my eyes, there he was, sitting on the grass looking out over the valley, I looked at him and felt as though somehow I knew him. I sat up and said hello. It was a bit like in a dream when you know that you know things even though there's no reason that you should. He turned and looked at me. All peaceful and quiet, he said, 'Greetings to you, most favoured one.' I laughed. My immediate thought was that he assumed I was someone else. Some high-born, rich princess kind of person, but I felt so at home with him immediately that I giggled and said, 'No, sorry, you've got the wrong person. I'm Mary. I just live up the hill in Nazareth.' He laughed, too. 'No, it's Mary I was looking for. It's you and God is with you.' I sat and looked at him for a minute and somehow I wasn't embarrassed to talk about God in a way that I usually wouldn't do. 'Well, I know,' I said. 'I love it out here. I feel as though I'm sitting with him, as though

I can lean my head on his shoulder and drink in the beauty of what he's made. It's just so beautiful. I feel sometimes as though God has done it just for me.' He smiled at me. Not in a conde-scending way as some people would, but as though he knew the secret, too. 'Yes, I know. He has,' he said. We laughed, and sat quietly for a minute, looking at the trees, the lambs in the distance, and the sweep of the valley. Then he turned to me again and said, 'God is with you in a very special way, Mary.' Something in the way he said it let me know that somehow this was really important, that I couldn't understand the depth of what it meant. I frowned. I began to think that he really had come looking for someone different, but already I knew that he hadn't. Then I began to think that maybe he wanted me to do something I wouldn't know how to do, but he reassured me: 'Do not be afraid, Mary, you have found favour with God.'

I almost laughed again in relief, except that he was so serious now. I knew, I knew that what he said was true, that somehow the God I knew out there on the hillside loved me deeply, loves us all like that. He is the kind of God that somehow wants to be with these little mortals he has made and delights in them, just as I had been delighting in the chicks and the catkins. I thought about the words 'highly favoured of God'. Well, I knew that I wasn't – no more than anyone else – and yet I knew that I was, too, because everyone is highly favoured! Somehow I knew that the ordinary, low-born of us, the village girls, were just as pre-cious to God as anyone else because that's what the God of Israel is like. Our history is full of ordinary people God has used. I've always loved those stories, identified with the men and women who knew that they were nothing, yet God loved being with them and making them something.

So, I sat quietly and waited to hear what he was going to say next. Who will ever believe it? He looked at me intently, yet very gently, and said, 'You will be with child and give birth to a son and you are to give him the name Jesus. He will be great and will be called the Son of the Most High.' If he hadn't been so serious, I might have laughed. I just stared at him. Part of me was so wanting to do whatever it was that this God of love might want and another part of me was astonished, speechless. Then I thought of Joseph and our wedding day still months away. 'How can I do that?' I said. 'I'm not even married yet.' He smiled at me. 'I know.' Something in the way he said it assured me that he did know, he knew all that mattered. He paused and then he said, 'God's Holy Spirit will come. The Most High will overshadow you.' The word he used was the one we sing in the psalms about being under God's wings, under his feathers, and I thought of the mother of those chicks and the way she would settle down over them. I smiled at the image, of God being like that with me and with a child who I would bear for him. It touched me deeply and there were tears in my eyes as I answered, 'Let it be done to me as you say.'

We were silent for a time, then he said, 'Your kinswoman Elizabeth is pregnant too. She who was barren for so long is already in her sixth month. Nothing is impossible with God. Her pregnancy, too, is holy.' I was delighted. Elizabeth. I knew now who I could tell about this indescribable encounter. I would go and see Elizabeth. She would believe me. She would know what to do.

'I am the handmaiden of the Lord,' I said. 'Let it be as you have told me.'

He gave me one last look, something of love, awe and joy all wrapped together. Then he disappeared. He did, just like that. That's how I knew. If I had ever wondered about it later and thought that I'd made it up and, really, he was a travelling storyteller, tricking me, that's how I knew that he was an angel. He was an angel sent from God to tell me that he, God of the heavens, truly wanted to make his home with us. Oh, what love is this! What a God! A God who comes to the humblest of us, the ordinary people of the villages. What a story. What an amazing plan, that he should overthrow the rich and the powerful and the important with a baby, born of a common village girl. I open my heart to him and somehow he creates these astounding riches, just like he creates beautiful poppies sprinkled through the wheat fields and the tiny pink cyclamens under the bank by the stream and the speckles on the pigeon's wing feathers. What a wonder.

My thoughts returned to Elizabeth. She's always been my favourite aunt. She's not really my aunt, but she's related to my mother and she's older than my mother so we call her aunt. We see a lot of her, even though she and her husband live down in the hills in Judea and we're up here in Nazareth. There's always been something special about her – maybe because she hadn't got any children – and she's always taken special notice of me. I love to go and stay with her and tell her things, what I dream about and things I wonder about, about God – everything really. She tells me things, too. I know how much she had hoped to have children and how hard it was for her to come to terms with not having any. So now the angel had told me that I was going to have a child and then that Elizabeth was already pregnant, almost in the same breath. I am so delighted. Elizabeth to have a baby! Me to have a baby! I wanted to go to her.

Somehow I managed to persuade my mother to let me go and I found someone heading down that way to travel with. All the way there I kept going over and over what the angel had said – that I would have a child, he was the Son of the Most High and he would have David's throne. My mind kept going back to the psalms that we sing together and the prophets' words, that one day God would rescue us from oppression, would show his compassion to us and would use the poor and the lowly. He had not forgotten Israel, he would not leave us to our enemies.

As we travelled, I began to sing the words of the psalms and the prophets' sayings, weaving them together to make a song of my own. It was a song about our God who comes to us – the ordinary ones, the poor and the humble, the ones who simply love him and wait for him and serve him just with our everyday lives.

My soul magnifies the Lord and my spirit rejoices in God my Saviour

Because he knows how small and undeserving I am, no better than anyone else. Yet now everyone is to be blessed by what he is doing through me!

The Most High God has done wonderful things for me, the Holy God of our fathers.

His compassion is poured out on those who know him and are in awe of him, through all of our ancestors' times and right into ours.

He has shown how powerful he is by using the poor and the lowly, as he always does!

The proud, the oppressors and the rulers and the conquerors – they do not impress him.

It is to us that he comes – the poor, the humble, those who have no claim to anything.

Those of us who hunger for him – it is to us that he comes. To those who think that they have everything – well, they don't need anything more than they have already.

He hasn't forgotten Israel and left us to our enemies. It is to us that he comes.

He has always cared for us and now, again, he is coming to us in a way that they will never guess – a hidden and secret way – bringing salvation through the least, as he always said to Abraham and all our fathers. He is coming to us.[1]

11

Imperfection – the human condition

Mary's gift to us was that she knew her becoming pregnant with the Christ was not because she deserved it, but because she was poor and humble and hungry for God – she understood the way of descent and the core of the Beatitudes. We, too, are called to bring forth the Christ in our lives.

Michael Leunig, an Australian cartoonist and poet, in his *A Common Prayer*, recognizes how difficult this process is:

> God be with the mother. As she carried her child may she carry her soul. As her child was born may she give birth and life and form to her own, higher truth. As she nourished and protected her child, may she nourish and protect her inner life and her independence. For her soul shall be her most painful birth, her most difficult child, and the dearest sister to her other children.[1]

I have found this to be one of the most difficult things to learn – to protect and nourish my inner being as I would my own child, how to show grace to myself. I am now convinced, however, that unless I have learned to live in this way I really haven't learned grace at all. Ah, yes, God's grace applies to others – the prodigal Father runs to his other sons, too – but what of myself? I still cling to trying to be the older brother, the one who earns God's love through my own self-righteousness, my own deservingness, and so it is clear that I have not truly learned grace. I cannot stop myself from thinking that, in the end, to get into heaven, the kingdom of heaven, I need to have got it right. How do I abandon all this and walk naked into the throne room of God, allowing my own brokenness to be seen?

Daniel Ladinsky, inspired by St John of the Cross, explores the idea of being 'pregnant with the holy' and bringing forth the sacred from our own being:

> The Virgin will come walking down the road pregnant with the holy, and say, 'I need shelter for the night, please take me inside your heart, my time is so close.' Then, under the roof of your soul, you will witness the sublime intimacy, the Divine, the Christ taking birth forever, as she grasps your hand for help, for each of us is the midwife of God, each of us. Yes there, under the dome of your being does creation come into existence eternally, through your womb, dear pilgrim – the sacred womb in your soul.[2]

The mothering of our own soul, our own inner being, is the path to maturity. It is only as we change our inner patterns of speech, learning to speak kindly to ourselves, that we truly live out grace. Only as I learn to show grace to myself, in the inner world of my own thoughts and reactions, can I become one who truly extends grace to others. As long as I am hard and judgemental about myself, others will intuit that harshness in my relationships with them. It is as we mother our own inner being that we learn to truly nurture others. Only then will we truly represent the God of grace to others around us. Most of us find it easier to be kind to others than we are to ourselves internally. Mostly we are able to focus more on the aspects of ourselves that we like, but try to cover, hiding them even from ourselves, the qualities that we see as negative or the parts we recognize as broken or failing.

John O'Donohue, an Irish poet and psychologist, explains:

> Our lives would be immeasurably enriched if we could but bring the same hospitality to meet the negative as we bring to the joyful and pleasurable . . . The negative is one of the closest friends of your destiny . . . You can only befriend the negative if you recognize that it is not destructive . . . One of your sacred duties is to exercise kindness towards [these qualities]. In a sense, you are called to be a loving parent to your delinquent qualities.[3]

Many of us have been convinced by a theology that calls us to be perfect, for a God who is perfect, and so we cannot see how we can come as broken ones – unless we quickly become 'whole'. Maybe it was OK to be broken and naked when we first repented, but now we must live righteously and cover our nakedness, leaving confessions to the addicted and the sinful. The 12-step programme of confession and interdependence is appropriate for them, we think, not us, and we hold on to our fig leaves of achievement and education.

Scott Peck, a psychiatrist and author of *The Road Less Travelled*, points out that acknowledgement of our brokenness is the only way – for all of us:

> Community requires the confession of brokenness. But how remarkable it is that in our culture brokenness must be 'confessed'. We think of confession as an act that should be carried out in secret, in the darkness of the confessional, with the guarantee of professional priestly or psychiatric confidentiality. Yet the reality is that every human being is broken and vulnerable. How strange that we should ordinarily feel compelled to hide our wounds when we are all wounded! Community requires the ability to expose our wounds and weaknesses to our fellow creatures. It also requires the ability to be affected by the wounds of others. But even more important is the LOVE that arises among us when we share, both ways, our woundedness.[4]

In my own journey, I have been finding that, indeed, I come closest to others and this God who accepts me, even delights in me, most deeply when I lay open my broken and vulnerable places. It happens when I dare to believe that I do not have to come in the fig leaves of my own goodness, but can trust grace to cover my nakedness. It happens when I accept that the shadow parts of myself need to be treated with kindness.

We thought that we were called to be perfect and righteous, like the 'Father who is perfect' in Matthew's version of the Sermon on the Mount.[5] In fact, that wording is a poor translation of the original. The Greek word *telos* is much more often translated as 'complete'.[6] *Telos* has to do with destiny, not perfection. So, instead, we are being called to a more honest way, a way where we walk with the merciful God, which is how Luke finishes his version of the parallel passage.[7]

Bennett Sims suggests that the phrase 'as your heavenly Father is perfect' actually lets us off the hook of perfectionism.[8] He says that God is clearly not a perfectionist – look at creation, look at Jesus' responses to events and people around him. So, if we are to be as God is in this, then we are not to be perfectionists, but, rather, 'conspicuously imperfect'. It is in our conspicuous imperfection, especially as leaders, that we let others see our dependence on God's grace, thus giving permission for others to be imperfect, too.

This, says Eberhard Arnold, of the Bruderhof Foundation, is the real perfection:

> Your life will have a kind of perfection, although you will not be a saint. The perfection will consist in this: you will be very weak and you will make many mistakes; you will be awkward, for you will be poor in spirit and hunger and thirst for justice. You will not be perfect, but you will love. This is the gate and the way. There is nothing greater than love. There is nothing more true than love, nothing more real. So let us hand our lives over to love and seal the bond of love.[9]

Our misunderstanding, thinking that God is calling us to faultless perfection, has caused many of us to hide our faults – from God, from each other and from ourselves. If we are to truly dance, we have to be able to know and acknowledge our imperfection – or this other kind of 'perfection' of which these writers speak.

In book after book, Henri Nouwen – very aware of his own brokenness and imperfection – focuses on our need to accept God's love and ourselves in our imperfection and brokenness. Nouwen was a priest and lecturer and author of over 40 books, translated into many languages. His *Life of the Beloved* explores the theme of brokenness:

> The leaders and prophets of Israel, who were clearly chosen and blessed, all lived very broken lives. And we, the

Beloved Sons and Daughters of God, cannot escape our brokenness either . . . Our brokenness is always lived and experienced as highly personal, intimate and unique. Yes, fearsome as it may sound, as the Beloved ones, we are called to claim our unique brokenness, just as we have to claim our unique chosenness and unique blessedness . . .[10]

Yes there is that voice, the voice that speaks from above and from within and that whispers softly or declares loudly: 'You are my Beloved, on you my favour rests.' It certainly is not easy to hear that voice in a world filled with voices that shout: 'You are no good; you are ugly; you are worthless; you are despicable; you are nobody – unless you can demonstrate the opposite.'

These negative voices are so loud and so persistent that it is easy to believe them. That's the great trap. It is the trap of self-rejection. Over the years I have come to realize that the greatest trap in our life is not success, popularity or power, but self-rejection. Success, popularity and power can indeed present a great temptation, but their seductive quality often comes from the way they are part of the much larger temptation to self-rejection.[11]

Nouwen explains that arrogance is our reaction against self-rejection, our striving to prove that we *are* worthy, but we need to overcome self-rejection in a different way, not just mask it, which is what arrogance does.

Self-rejection is the greatest enemy of the spiritual life because it contradicts the sacred voice that calls us the 'Beloved'. Becoming the Beloved is the great spiritual journey we have to make . . . Becoming the Beloved means letting the truth of our Belovedness become enfleshed in everything we think, say and do. It entails a long and painful process of appropriation or, better, incarnation.[12]

This idea of incarnation – learning to live out who God has declared us to be as a human being – involves daily, even moment by moment, choices to see God as the Lover and myself as the Beloved. The writers who help us with this most are those who have struggled with their own imperfection and have learned to accept themselves as a mix of wholeness and brokenness, of light and dark, as all humans are. Poetry and stories are frequently the best ways to explore these mysteries, these paradoxes.

Gerard Manley Hopkins, a Jesuit poet who also struggled with his own sexuality, wrote the famous 'Pied Beauty' – a poem that praises God for 'all things counter':

> Glory be to God for dappled things . . .
> All things counter, original, spare, strange,
> Whatever is fickle, freckled . . .
> He fathers-forth.[13]

Hopkins concludes that not only is creation dappled but also each human being. The expectation is that we will become, at last, in spite of our fallenness, 'immortal diamond'. Yet, somehow, now, even in human form, while still a 'poor potsherd', we are immortal diamonds.

> I am all at once what Christ is, since he is what I am,
>   and
> This Jack, joke, poor potsherd, patch, matchwood,
>   immortal diamond,
> Is immortal diamond.[14]

Hopkins knows that this is his only hope of fulfilling his longing to be 'perfect'. Both he and Nouwen have discovered that the spiritual journey is one of paradox – what James Fowler[15] calls 'the sacrament of defeat', which is that our own failure is indeed the means of grace.

Earlier on in our spiritual journeys we expect truth to be certain and the way that we should live to be plain. As life goes on, however, and we meet with triumph and disaster, defeat and brokenness, we find a deeper reality. Then we reach the point where we are more open to 'the truth in apparent contradictions' and find life to be, in the words of Louis MacNeice's poem 'Entirely',[16] 'a prism' in which joy and pain are mixed together.

There is a story told of Francis of Assisi, who many of us may consider to be as close to perfection as a human can be. The story, though, shows that his understanding of 'perfection' is one of being poor in spirit, of being in love, of accepting our undeservingness, our imperfection, our humanness, and simply letting it go.

One day Saint Francis and Brother Leo were walking down the road. Noticing that Leo was depressed, Francis turned and asked: 'Leo, do you know what it means to be pure of heart?'

'Of course. It means to have no sins, faults or weaknesses to reproach myself for.'

'Ah,' said Francis, 'now I understand why you're sad. We will always have something to reproach ourselves for . . . The sadness of not being perfect, the discovery that you really are sinful, is a feeling much too human, even borders on idolatry . . . Accept being shipwrecked . . . See only the compassion, the infinite patience, and the tender love of Christ . . . That suffices.'[17]

We need to see that God is enough. No attempt at perfection, achievement, progress, human relationship will fulfil the deepest longing of the human heart. I cannot satisfy my own standards, nor the expectations of anyone else, except by surrendering to this reality.

12

Surrendering what people think – the only way to true relationship

Ever since God said 'It is not good for the man to be alone',[1] we have lived in the paradox of being individuals made for God alone and humans who are part of relationships. Much has been written on independence, codependence, interdependence and on differences between people and the ways in which they relate to each other – introversion, extroversion, schizoid tendencies and so on. Somehow each one of us has to find out how to live in relationships and yet alone 'inside our own heads', in community and yet apart as we are made for God alone. It is a mystery. The likelihood is that, for all of our lives, each of us will be dancing between being too alone and too close, too dependent and too independent, too easily hurt and too insensitive.

It is a characteristic of the lives of many of the mystics that they seem somehow to find a balance point in this complex dance. The place of balance seems to be that of giving their hearts wholly to the Divine and then somehow also to other people.

Mother Teresa, our modern-day mystic, found the face of Christ in the destitute and dying, so could give to them as to a lover. Having given herself to God, being willing to find herself in him, she could then give freely to others. Thus, it is not a balance in the sense that we give a certain amount of ourselves to God and a certain amount to people. Rather, it is giving and finding ourselves in God and then being free to give fully in our human relationships. It is giving fully to others but without the awful underlying heart-need that says, 'Give! Give!' and is never satisfied.[2]

Those of us who are people of the heart are always, in a sense, on the take. We have the wonderful gift of wanting to move towards others, but, hidden deeply in that, often from ourselves, is our own heart, crying out for love. That hunger is fed by the love other people show us, their interest and care. That is as it should be, but, for most of us, it is not enough – we hunger for more people to value us or we long for our lovers and friends to show just that much more love and understanding. Our hearts remain hungry. Thus, when we read the words of a mystic or saint, saying, 'God, you are enough for me', we feel that only a saint can say such things as they are a little removed from the reality of being human.

Julian of Norwich, a mystic of the Middle Ages, was one such. Actually, we don't even know her real name. She lived in a room built within or against the walls of a small church called St Julian's, near the river in Norwich, England, and so is called Julian. It is said that she would have a window open so that she could listen to and counsel passers-by.

When she was only 30, she became ill, was believed to be dying, and she had such a vision of God, of the passion of Christ, that it sustained her for decades afterwards – and, through her writings, others in the centuries since. From out of this vision came her oft-quoted words of comfort: 'All shall be well, and all manner of thing shall be well.'[3] There is still a church on the site of the original church in Norwich – rebuilt since Julian's time, and rebuilt again since the bombings of the Second World War. A room has also been built where she would have lived and there her words are written: 'Thou art enough for me.'

I, an ordinary woman of the twenty-first century, have wondered how to reach the place where I would be able to say those words. At times have thought that I, too, would somehow have to reach saintly status first. Since childhood I have sung the words of the hymn 'Take my life and let it be consecrated Lord to thee, take my will and make it thine, it shall be no longer mine . . .',[4] but how does this work out in real life, every day? Especially, how is the longing of my heart to be quenched when it feels like it is human love that I want most? Many times I have said to God, 'God, it is you that I want' and, every now and then, it will feel as though that is true. Most of the time, though, I live the ordinary human experience of part of me longing for God and part of me wanting human love and believing it to be the only thing that will fulfil my deepest desire.

Part of that longing is simply wanting to be loved, but part of it, too, is caring what other people think of me. If someone loves me or, even, is in love with me, then I must be lovable. Such is the logic of the human heart. Such, indeed, is the role of infancy and childhood – that the child, knowing herself loved, can grow up with a sense of her love-worthiness, which happens not because of anything she does, but simply because she is.

The deep longing to be loved, particularly romantically, is the subject of another chapter. Before exploring the specifics of desire and romantic love, however, it is important to recognize here the part of desire that is more simply about caring what other people think of me. This is an addiction for many of us, an obsession with wondering what people think, going over what they have said or might have meant. I have explored it by borrowing Mark's story of the rich young ruler, but have changed it to fit my own experience of the one thing I needed.[5]

One day a woman of good standing in the community came and knelt before him and said, 'Good teacher, what must I do to best serve your kingdom?'

He said to her, 'Why do you measure who is good and who is not? Only God is good – God alone.'

She puzzled in her heart at this because she wanted to be good.

Then he said to her, 'If you want to choose life, live in God's presence, do what the scriptures teach.'

She answered, 'Beloved, all this I have tried to do since childhood.'

He, looking on her, loved her, looked into her eyes and said with great love, 'Still, there is one thing that you need to do if you want to enter into life fully. Give away all of what people think of you.'

She was silent, for she cared much. 'Aaron, Allan, Anne, Bernie, Brian, Charles, Chris, Christine, David . . . through to . . . Zac, Zena.'

Then she looked long into his eyes and answered, 'Jesus, it is you that I want. It is only what you think of me that matters. Help me to give it all to you until I am fully surrendered, fully free.'

They sat in silence for a long time. Then she said, 'Jesus, my heart is sore. Why is this?'

He answered, 'You have given them each something of your heart and it is not theirs to keep it for you. If you give your heart wholly to me, I will hold it for you – tenderly, carefully, lovingly, kindly.'

She said, 'I take it back gently, from each of those to whom I have given it. I place it in your hands and yours alone. I trust your love.'

In the original story, Jesus names riches as the one thing that the young man needed to give away. Whatever the 'one thing' is for each of us, it is the surrendering of it that brings life. Anthony de Mello explains that, if we look carefully, we will see that there is one thing that causes unhappiness. He calls that one thing an attachment. An attachment is a belief that, without something, we are not going to be happy. It is an emotional state of clinging caused by the belief that without that particular thing or person we cannot be happy.[6]

As the story above names the attachment that I have held on to, I shall surrender something else that will bring me another step closer to being able to say, 'You are enough for me.' What it is that I want to surrender is something that is repeated in my moment by moment thought life when my mind returns to an incident that has happened that day or that month or years ago and tries to reconceptualize it so that I come out looking a little better – so the other person will think that much better of me. This is an addiction that needs to be healed. As with most addictions, it is in the moment of longing, that moment of catching myself revisiting in this way, that I need to choose instead to give the person to God, to give what they think of me to God, and say, 'Beloved, it is you I want, it is what you think of me that matters.' This is the kind of surrender that leads to freedom.

Ignatius of Loyola has a prayer that I often repeat – just to remind myself how completely I want to be free and that the God of love is enough for me:

Take, Lord, and receive all my liberty, my memory, my understanding, and my entire will, all that I have and possess. You have given it all to me. To you, Lord, I return it. All of it is yours: dispose of it wholly according to your will. Give me only your love and your grace, and that will be enough for me.[7]

Why are we afraid to pray such a prayer? Are we afraid that awful things might happen to us if we do? We are entirely in the hands of the Creator anyway. It is only an illusion that we are our own, independent beings. Jesus told us that, by worrying, we cannot lengthen our lives.[8] Returning to God what is in God's hands anyway is lining ourselves up with the flow of the universe.

Sometimes we may be afraid that such a prayer, such a stance, will make us so other-worldly that we will be of no earthly good, out of touch with reality, and may somehow distance ourselves from the people and needs around us. This is not the experience of the mystics. Ignatius, who wrote the prayer we have just read, is known for his service to others and his founding of the Society of Jesus, which has schools, hospitals and other institutions all around the world – frequently where there is great need.

It seems that, like Mother Teresa, surrendering our hearts to God gives us freedom to find Christ in other people. Daniel Ladinsky interprets the Persian mystic Shams-ud-din Muhammad Hafiz as saying:

> My eyes, my eyes can no longer hide the wondrous fact
> of who you really are
> The Beautiful One whom I adore
> Has pitched His royal tent inside of you,
> So I will always lean my heart
> As close to your soul
> As I can.[9]

13

The deeper desire

The longing for connection is a core aspect of humanness and one that is often seen as fraught with opportunities for imperfection. That longing is central to our understanding of the spiritual journey. It has been suggested that there are three main pictures or metaphors that characterize the human spiritual journey and one of these fits particularly well with our own experiences and way of being.[1]

The first of the three pictures or metaphors is the hero's journey, characterized by action, adventure, conquest and sacrifice – slaying dragons and rescuing maidens. Some of us find God in that kind of journey.

The second is the journey of suffering, which certainly seems to be thrust on some and becomes for them a sacrament of grace – the way to the Divine. The book of Job is an example of this kind of journey from the Bible, Job saying, after enduring his unbelievable suffering, 'I have uttered what I did not understand . . . but now my eye sees thee.'[2]

The third is the way of the lover – struggling with the longing for connection, intimacy, wanting to know and be known, or with a longing for sexual connection. Those who deeply yearn for these things usually see a person or a relationship as being the object of that feeling, but the way of desire, the journey of the lover, is, most deeply, ultimately, a longing for the Divine. That longing may lead us into byways and errors, but is, in the end, a God-given and profoundly good desire. That is because, if we stay with it, follow it truly, it will finally lead us to not only our true selves but also to the Divine Beloved.

The anonymous fourteenth-century author of *The Cloud of Unknowing*[3] puts joy and desire together:

So abounding will that [joyful enthusiasm] be that it will follow you to bed at night and rise with you in the morning. It will pursue you through the day in everything you do ... The enthusiasm and the desire will seem to be part of each other; so much so, that you will think it is only one desire you feel, though you will be at a loss to say just precisely what it is you long for. Your whole personality will be transformed; your countenance will radiate an inner beauty; and for as long as you feel it nothing will sadden you.

Recognizing the depth of our desire can lead us to believe that our longing will always be unrequited, but it is the expectation of this anonymous mystic that the desire and the joy will come together, that in the deepest place there will be something that is requited, that is fulfilled. We may not be able to name what it is we long for, yet, at its deepest, the longing is a God-given longing, which, in the end, can become at one with a joy that follows us to bed at night and rises with us in the morning. The mystics – the men and women who seem to have found an experiential and deep relationship with God – insist that our longing finds its very source in God. Janet Ruffing, a spiritual director explains:

Our desiring already originates in God desiring us ... [The mystics] strongly assert that our desires, our wants, our longings, our outward and inward searching – when uncovered, expressed and recognized – all lead to the Divine Beloved at the core. As Augustine so tellingly phrased it in the *Confessions*, 'Our hearts are restless until they rest in you, O God.'[4]

If that longing really has its origin in God's longing for us, then what may have seemed to us a sin or, at best, a temptation, may be a gift – for it leads to the one who longs for relationship more intensely than we do. Philip Yancey, in fact, suggests that the Bible reveals a God who is 'hopelessly in love' with us.[5]

Ruffing suggests that using our longing as a way to find God necessitates identifying the desire beneath the desire. First, though, doing so, obliges us to stay with our desire, however painful, in order to go beneath it: 'I am convinced that many Christians never entertain their desires long enough to know what they really want. If we habitually suppress our wants,' she says (and, I would add, or habitually smother them with false comfort), 'we may not discover the true core of our longing that could lead us deeply into God.'[6]

Many of us have a distorted understanding of desire. We may have grown up as Christians or become Christians along the way and have this idea that what we truly want will not be what God wants. We think that God will want to send us to some inhospitable place to do something that is particularly difficult and painful. What Ruffing is suggesting here instead is that if we stay with what we truly want, we will find God's desire for us. We, though, have so often put our desires aside, fearing to identify them, not daring to get in touch with them. Ruffing suggests that we do the following exercise:

> When was the last time you asked yourself what you really want? And how long did you allow yourself to entertain that longing? Thirty seconds, a couple of minutes? What inner or outer voices suggested that, whatever it was, you ought not to be so foolish as to think it could be satisfied? At some point did you judge yourself wilful or selfish?[7]

We judge our desires to be wilful, selfish or – and I am sure this is true for many of us – downright sinful. It is important that we take some time to identify what we really desire, to articulate it, because, underneath it, is a longing for connection with the divine other. We want the experience of knowing and being known, being recognized and valued for our most true self. Any desire, if we allow it to take us deep enough, will lead us to the one who made us. The longing in us is, ultimately, for God.

The longing and falling short, then almost giving up out of disappointment, is captured in the following poem by Shams-ud-din Muhammad Hafiz:

> You have not danced so badly, my dear,
> Trying to hold hands with the Beautiful One.

The deeper desire

You have waltzed with great style,
My sweet, crushed angel,
To have ever neared God's Heart at all.

Our partner is notoriously difficult to follow,
And even His best musicians are not always easy to
hear . . .
But [I] know the Beloved's eternal habits.
Have patience, for he will not be able to resist your
longing for long.

You have not danced so badly, my dear,
Trying to kiss the Beautiful One.
You have actually waltzed with tremendous style,
O my sweet, O my sweet, crushed angel.[8]

The line 'Have patience, for he will not be able to resist your longing for long' suggests, again, that our longing originates in God, so God's true desire is to respond to us. God himself has placed that longing in our hearts, so, if we can stay with the longing and the pain of it, we will find our way to God, who, in fact, is taking the initiative in coming towards us. It is not just human desire and humans trying to reach the Divine, it is the Divine reaching out for us.

The initiative God takes, moving towards us, is the essence of Christian understanding:

This movement of the Mystery towards us forms the core meaning of revelation in Christian faith. God awakens us to this divine–human love affair and initiates in us the search for the Divine Beloved. No matter how confusedly we interpret this experience, no matter how many mistakes we make along the way, no matter how often this love for the Divine Beloved gets displaced onto other loves or other objects of desire, God continues to solicit and elicit our love. As Sebastian Moore says 'All desire [is] solicitation by the mystery we are in . . . all human loves contribute to our capacity for this divine–human intimacy.[9]

The assurance that, 'no matter how often this love for the Divine Beloved gets displaced onto other loves or other

85

objects of desire', God continues to try to draw us to him, is the message implicit in the parable of the prodigal son. Indeed, it is implicit in the gospel story, the core revelation of God's word.

One of the reasons for our tendency to misdirect our love towards objects of desire other than God is that we cannot bear the pain of unfulfilled desire. We prefer almost anything to the sense of emptiness we are left with when we know that our desire has not been satisfied. Henri Nouwen, in his own struggle with longing for connection and intimacy, wrote to himself:

> What is your pain? It is the experience of not receiving what you most need. It is a place of emptiness where you feel sharply the absence of the love you most desire. To go back to that place is hard, because you are confronted there with your wounds as well as with your powerlessness to heal yourself. You are so afraid of that place that you think of it as a place of death. Your instinct for survival makes you run away and go looking for something else that can give you a sense of at-homeness, even though you know full well that it can't be found out in the world.
>
> You have to begin to trust that your experience of emptiness is not the final experience, that beyond it is a place where you are being held in love. As long as you do not trust that place beyond your emptiness, you cannot safely re-enter the place of pain.[10]

Being able to stay with our pain, our emptiness, our longing, is the key to finding the presence of God. 'Blessed', says the first Beatitude, 'are the poor'[11] – those who know that they are in need. 'Blessed are those who hunger and thirst' is a message implicit in Jesus' sayings. If we can only stay with our thirst long enough, we will find the most fulfilling quenching in the one who brings living water. It is those who deny their thirst or drink shallow, non-living water who do not find the true water of life.

Simone Weil, a French Christian philosopher and activist, explains that we need to recognize our hunger specifically:

> In the period of preparation for loving God, the soul loves in emptiness. It does not know whether anything real

answers its love. It may believe that it knows, but to
believe is not to know. Such a belief does not help. The
soul knows for certain only that it is hungry. The important thing is that it announces its hunger by crying. A
child does not stop crying if we suggest to it that perhaps
there is no such thing as bread. It goes on crying just
the same. The danger is not lest the soul should doubt
whether there is bread, but lest, by a lie, it should persuade itself that it is not hungry. It can only persuade
itself of this by lying, for the reality of its hunger is not a
belief, it is a certainty.[12]

John Eldredge addresses this idea in his book, *Journey of Desire*.[13]
Eldredge is involved in the men's movement, so is concerned with
men's lives and helping them to recognize that they, too, desire
an intimate relationship with God. Many times when we talk
about desire and images of desire, it is easier for women to
put that image and their image of God together. In the picture
of the lover and beloved in the Song of Songs, many women
find that they can identify with the beloved bride and the
divine lover searching for her. Men sometimes find that harder
to identify with and do not know how to respond, particularly
as our emphasis is on God as male. We have tended to perpetu-
ate that male image, even though there are numbers of images
in the Bible of God as feminine. Men, therefore, may well
find Eldredge's book is particularly helpful in overcoming
this problem.

He tells the story of a sea lion lost in the desert with only a
small pool, dreaming of the sea. The sea lion wonders whether
his dreams of the sea are only in his imagination and almost
gives up his longing for it – 'lying to its soul', as Weil put it. Then
comes the thwarting – the spoiling of the lesser thing that each
of us chooses instead of our greater desire to try to satisfy it.
That is, the idea that God may indeed get in the way of our more
superficial desires in order to stir up in us a hunger for the deeper
journey, the deeper desire within us.

Some people seem to be satisfied with very little or else are
good at convincing themselves that they are. Rainer Maria Rilke
suggests that there are some who 'live carelessly . . . Smoothly

reaching high rank', yet it is 'those who thirst . . . who cling to you for life' God takes pleasure in.

> You see I want so much.
> Maybe I want everything:
> the darkness of each unending fall
> and the sparkling light of each ascent.
>
> So many live carelessly
> wanting nothing,
> smoothly reaching high rank
> through slick negotiation.
>
> But you rejoice in the faces of those who thirst.
> You delight in all who cling to you for life.
>
> You are not dead yet, and it is not too late
> to plunge into your pregnant depths
> where life reveals its secret presence.[14]

We plunge into the depths of our own being to find God's presence. Rilke notices, as most mystics seem to, that, in reality, desire and pain often come together. John Eldredge's sea lion story illustrates that the desert experience is the means to finding God. Rilke highlights that it is those who thirst who will find the presence of the Spirit within. The Song of Songs points out that the desert experience results in the lover leaning on her beloved.[15] This idea has been recognized right the way through the Christian tradition.

For many men and women in our culture, the peak of desire and longing is found in romance. Robert Johnson has explored this in his book *We: The psychology of romantic love*: 'Romantic love is the single greatest energy system in the Western psyche. In our culture it has supplanted religion as the arena in which men and women seek meaning, transcendence, wholeness, and ecstasy.'[16] As a society, we have not yet learned to handle the tremendous power of romantic love. We turn it into tragedy and alienation as often as we turn it into enduring human relationships.[17]

To explore that transcendent desire of romantic love, Robert Johnson uses the myth of Tristan and Iseult (in other versions called Tristram and Isolde): 'It is one of the most moving, most beautiful and tragic of all the great epic tales. It was the first story in Western literature that dealt with romantic love. It is the source from which all our romantic literature has sprung, from *Romeo and Juliet* down to the love story in the movie at the local cinema . . . It shows a man torn among the conflicting forces and loyalties that rage within the male psyche when he is consumed by the joys, the passions, and the sufferings of romance.'[18]

14

Tristan and Iseult

The story of Tristan and Iseult dates from the time of the Grail myths, around the twelfth century. The stories of this time tell of noble knights who slay dragons, rescue maidens and embark on quests, proving their loyalty to their king and, maybe, to a princess or other high-born lady.

Loyalty to a lady at that time did not involve a romantic or sexual relationship, but, rather, it was one of devotion and service. It is from this time, however, that romances became not just lyrical stories, as in the original sense of the word, but 'romantic', with the meaning that we attach to the word today. The story of Tristan and Iseult marks this change from a tale of a knight merely serving his queen to that of him falling in love with her. Tristan's devotion to his king results in a romance with Iseult that begins during her journey from Ireland to be queen.

King Mark lived in Cornwall. Tristan had left his father's kingdom to seek challenges and attempt great deeds and so had joined the court of his mother's brother, King Mark, to whom he swore allegiance. However, King Mark had not married and had no heir. As a result, some of the other knights began to be jealous of Tristan, believing that he was being favoured and even groomed to take King Mark's place when the time came. However, King Mark was advised that he should marry and produce heirs as they would be recognized by all his subjects. He resisted the idea at first but then agreed that, if the lady from whose head the beautiful golden red hair that had been dropped by a swallow on his windowsill could be found, he would marry her. Tristan volunteered to take to sea with this band of followers and go where fortune led them in search of this lady.

Storms blew them to the shores of neighbouring Ireland. As a result of further adventures and the slaying of a dragon that was wreaking destruction on Ireland, Tristan won the hand of Iseult, the princess, and so gained her father's agreement that she marry his king.

Everything was going according to plan until the ship was becalmed one day before reaching Cornwall. There was a nearby beach and the ships' crew and other servants made the most of the sunny weather, enjoying themselves, roaming the fields and woods, while they waited for the wind to pick up again. Tristan and Iseult stayed on board and became engaged in conversation. As the day became hotter, they looked for food and drink. Finding a pitcher of wine, they poured themselves a drink. Unbeknown to them, Iseult's mother had given a love potion to Iseult's handmaiden, Brangien. She was to give it to the bride on her marriage night so that Iseult and King Mark would fall in love and enjoy a happy life together. Instead, Iseult unknowingly drank the love potion with Tristan.

> The Queen drank deep of that draught and gave it to Tristan and he drank also long and emptied it all.
>
> Brangien came in upon them; she saw them gazing at each other in silence as though ravished and apart; she saw before them the pitcher standing there . . . and cried aloud: '. . . Iseult, my friend, and Tristan, you, you have drunk death together.'
>
> . . . But it seemed to Tristan as though an ardent briar, sharp-thorned but with flower most sweet smelling, drave roots into his blood and laced the lovely body of Iseult all round about it and bound it to his own and to his every thought and desire.'[1]

Inexorably, irrevocably, they fall in love with each other, experiencing the 'fatal bands of love'[2] twining their hearts together. Both remained loyal to the wishes of their realms, however, and Tristan nobly delivered Iseult to the palace. Before they parted, though, the lovers exchanged promises (and, later, rings), and vowed that, if one ever needed the other, they would have only to send the ring and the other would come.

The royal marriage went ahead. There follows a long story of love and betrayal, loyalty and deception. Although the potency of the love potion is meant to wear off after three years, the two lovers secretly meet, refuelling their feelings for each other. Eventually, Tristan goes to France and marries another, but, even then, he cannot let go of his beloved Iseult, so his marriage is undermined by deception. Years pass and still the lovers long to be together.

Most of us in the West have this kind of romantic yearning deeply embedded in our psyche. Even though we may be critical of these lovers for their deception and destructive choices, something in us still identifies with their longing to be together and justifies their willingness to sacrifice all for 'true love'. We understand, at a heart level, that the pursuit of true love somehow excuses any behaviour.

When Tristan becomes seriously ill, he sends his ring with a servant who sails to England to find Iseult and he hopes that she will come to him, believing that her coming may enable him to live again. Having followed the story so far, we can understand why Tristan does this. However, we also understand the behaviour of Tristan's wife, when she reacts in broken-hearted anger on realizing that Tristan has sent his ring to Iseult. She overheard the conversation in which Tristan instructed the servant who sailed to fetch Iseult, telling him that if the Queen is with him when he returns, to sail into port with a white sail. If, however, she has refused to come, he must hoist a black sail so that Tristan will know as soon as possible whether his beloved has come or not. Meanwhile, Tristan waited 'and day by day he sent watchers to the shore to see if some ship came, and to learn the colour of her sail. There was no other thing left in his heart.'[3]

Matthew Arnold's retelling of the story shows how we understand that a kiss, romantic love itself, which 'binds our souls', is the source of life and healing:

> . . . but where
> Is that other Iseult fair,
> That proud, first Iseult, Cornwall's queen?
> She, whom Tristram's ship of yore
> From Ireland to Cornwall bore,
> To Tyntagel, to the side
> Of King Marc, to be his bride?
> She who, as they voyaged, quaff'd
> With Tristram that spiced magic draught,
> Which since then for ever rolls
> Through their blood, and binds their souls . . .

One such kiss as those of yore
Might thy dying knight restore!
Does the love-draught work no more?
Art thou cold, or false, or dead,
Iseult of Ireland?[4]

As the day nears for the expected return of the boat, Tristan, near to death and unable to rise from his bed, asks his wife to watch for the little sailing ship. Knowing now why he asks and who he is waiting for, she watches to see if his lover will come. She eventually sees the long-awaited ship. Tristan, hovering between death and life, asks her what the colour of the sail is. His wife, out of her own hurt and grief, lies to him and says that it is black. In fact, it is white – signalling that Iseult is on board, but Tristan dies, believing Iseult has not come to him. Iseult arrives too late and, on hearing of her beloved's death, also dies, heart-broken.

'Love, you sent for me, and I came,' she said. 'I am too late to bring you back, but I can go with you, and so we shall be parted no more.'[5] Roses spring up from each of their graves and entwine, commemorating their love.

15

Romance, sexuality and spirituality

In the mythical story, Tristan and Iseult's love for each other becomes worship. They have the belief that only the other can give them life, that death is better than life without their beloved. This is an inner belief that we in the West have inherited with our culture. The story shows the shift from the ideal being spiritual to the seeking of earthly fulfilment of this other-worldly longing.

Woven into this tragic love story is the merging together of courtly love and sexual romance. Robert Johnson explains that, previously, there had been 'courtly love', which was love at a distance, on a spiritual level: 'the model was the brave knight who worshipped a fair lady as his inspiration, the symbol of all beauty and perfection, the ideal, that moved him to be noble, spiritual, refined, and high-minded.'[1] Due to the Tristan and Iseult myth and the stories that have followed it, there has been a movement away from the spiritual and towards a personalizing and sexualizing of these ideals: 'In our time we have mixed courtly love into our sexual relationships and marriages, but we still hold the medieval belief that true love has to be the ecstatic adoration of a man or woman who carries, for us, the image of perfection.'[2] Johnson shows that, in our culture, we have come to see the romantic–sexual relationship as the one that should somehow make us whole: 'As a mass phenomenon, romantic love is peculiar to the West[3] . . . This is a psychological phenomenon that is very specific. When we are "in love" we believe we have found the ultimate meaning in life, reified in another human being. We feel we are finally completed.'[4]

Johnson makes it very clear that our longing is to experience sexuality, especially when mixed with romance, as a peak experience. We long for something to complete us, to give meaning to our lives. As a culture, we have shifted our gaze from a transcendent God to personal romantic–sexual relationships. Johnson calls this the great wound of the Western psyche – the expectation that individual relationships will bring us fulfilment. He suggests that it is only in facing this and embracing the pain of moving through it that we will develop into more whole beings and a healthier culture will result.

In contrast to this romantic wounding, Origen, an early father of the Church (185–254 AD), talks of the 'wound of love' as the soul's desire for God.[5] David Downing, in his exploration of C. S. Lewis' understanding of joy, expresses it thus: ' "the wound of love" [describes] the intense longing of the soul bride for Christ the bridegroom.'[6] What these authors are recognizing is that we, as humans, have an intense longing for intimacy, union, transcendence. It is a wound of love that Origen perceived to be a spiritual longing for the Divine, but which the West has come to view as a romantic, sexual yearning. It is as though we have misunderstood the dance with God, thinking that any dance and any dance partner will suffice.

In naming our desire, we are able to move beyond it. In acknowledging the deep longing of romantic, sexual love, we can accept other people as human, not divine, and find that God is the answer to the deeper longing underlying what we have interpreted as being a romantic, sexual longing.

Every committed couple faces this challenge. It involves accepting that their partner – the one they have fallen in love with and are expecting to fulfil their heart's desires – is human, not divine, and so their love needs to change from ecstatic worship to a more grounded, committed love. This does not mean that we should repress and deny sexuality, as the Church traditionally has done, but, rather, acknowledge and accept ourselves as sexual beings so that we can come into the presence of God more completely.

The Bible itself has various stories that tell us things about sexuality and romance. Sex is not hidden away as it has been in much of Church history. The power of sexual attraction is certainly named – the stories of David and Bathsheba, Samson and Delilah are known by many who have never even thought of reading the Bible. There is another story that is less well known and shows how potent and capricious sexual desire can be. It is the story of Amnon, David's son, and his half-sister by one of David's other wives.

> In the course of time, Amnon, son of David, fell in love with Tamar, the beautiful sister of Absalom, son of David. Amnon became frustrated to the point of illness on account of his sister Tamar, for she was a virgin, and it seemed impossible for him to do anything to her . . . So Amnon lay down and pretended to be ill. When the king came to see him, Amnon said to him, 'I would like my sister Tamar to come and make some special bread in my sight, so that I may eat from her hand.' . . . But when she took it to him to eat, he grabbed her and said, 'Come to bed with me, my sister.' 'Don't, my brother!' she said to him . . . But he refused to listen to her, and since he was stronger than she, he raped her. Then Amnon hated her with intense hatred. In fact, he hated her more than he had loved her. Amnon said to her, 'Get up and get out!'[7]

This story is simply included among the others about David's life. It is part of the journey of Absalom towards his attempt to take the kingdom away from David. In his anger, Absalom plots and kills Amnon, his half-brother, two years after the rape.

Thus, it can be seen that the Bible does not try to hide the strength of sexual desire, nor the weaknesses of human beings. However, neither does it make sexual sin out to be unforgivable. Solomon, to whom God grants the gift of wisdom, is the son of David and Bathsheba. Solomon, presumably, writes the beautiful love song that is the Song of Songs, which we have kept as part of our scriptures. The book is specifically sexual and sets sexual love squarely inside human and spiritual reality.

> O that you would kiss me with the kisses of your mouth!
> For your love is better than wine . . .
> Draw me after you, let us make haste.
> The king has brought me into his chambers . . .
> Behold, you are beautiful my love . . . you are beautiful.[8]

These verses can be thought of as purely sexual or purely spiritual and, indeed, many Bible commentaries have opted for one or the other of these interpretations. Alternatively, we can understand that it is more complex than that and sexuality is a God-given gift for ecstatic union as well as being a metaphor for our relationship with the Divine Beloved.

Paul encompasses both interpretations, bringing together the earthly marriage relationship and the bride of Christ metaphor: 'For this reason a man will leave his father and mother and be united to his wife, and the two will become one flesh. This is a profound mystery – but I am talking about Christ and the Church. However, each one of you also must love his wife as he loves himself.'[9] Paul is thus talking about both levels of union – married sexuality and the union of human beings with our God. 'It is a profound mystery', he says, acknowledging the complexity and difficulty that humans have with these matters.

When we struggle to understand, we tend to make myths – stories that often contain magical elements to help us cope with the power and complexity of the ideas we are struggling with. In the story of Tristan and Iseult, there are a number of magical events – the central one being the drinking of the magic potion. We understand, because the potion is magical, that Tristan and Iseult 'cannot help' being in love, even when Iseult was promised to, then married, someone else. We can excuse them because the potion is magic, so they are unable to resist it. This is our human way of struggling to come to grips with the potency of sexual desire and romantic longing.

Rosemary Sutcliff, author of many books written for teenagers that are set in historic Britain, creates her stories using myths and historical details, but tries to make them true to life, so that we can identify with the characters as being really like us. She tells the story of Tristan and Iseult without the magic potion and, in the foreword to the book, explains why:

In all the versions that we know, Tristan and Iseult fall in love because they accidentally drink together a love potion which was meant for Iseult and her husband King Marc on their wedding night. Now the story of Tristan and Iseult is basically the same as two other great Celtic love stories, Diarmid and Grania, and Deirdre and the sons of Usna, and in neither of them is there any suggestion of a love potion. I am sure in my own mind that the medieval story-tellers added it to make an excuse for Tristan and Iseult for being in love with each other when Iseult was married to somebody else. And for me, this turns something that was real and living and part of themselves into something artificial, the result of drinking a sort of magic drug. So I have left out the love potion.[10]

Sutcliff is helping us face the reality of human sexuality – as the Bible story of Amnon and Tamar does. Amnon did not drink a magic potion, he was not under a spell – that is the reality of sexual desire. So, when Sutcliff tells of Tristan and Iseult falling in love, she uses the catalyst of touch and romantic imagery and helps the reader to identify with the sexual–romantic longing that has become part of our culture.

Now this was the first time that ever they had touched each other, save for the times when the Princess had tended Tristan's wounds, and that was a different kind of touching; and as he set her down, their hands came together as though they did not want it to be so quickly over. And standing hand in hand, they looked at each other, and for the first time Tristan saw that the Princess's eyes were deeply blue, the colour of wild wood-columbines; and she saw that his were as grey as the restless water out beyond the headland. And they were so close that each saw their own reflection standing in the other one's eyes; and in that moment it was as though something of Iseult entered into Tristan and something of Tristan into Iseult, that could never be called back again for as long as they lived.[11]

By inheriting Western culture, we have absorbed these ambiguous responses and beliefs about romance and sexuality. We accept the potency of sexual desire, we long for a romantic–sexual union to bring us into an experience of fulfilment, yet we have separated it from spirituality, the true peak of human ecstasy. We may be able to acknowledge that, in lesser areas, staying with our desire will bring us eventually to the Divine, but it is more difficult to believe that staying present in sexual desire can also bring us into deeper relationship with our Creator God.

The story of Jesus meeting with the woman at the well shows an interaction that revolves around sexuality, desire and brokenness. The woman had had five husbands and the man she was living with at the time she met Jesus was not her husband. In my reading of the story, she knows that she has used her sexuality to try and meet her deep needs and continues to do so. I am sure Jesus was aware of that, but was unfazed by it. I do not believe that that was because he saw sexuality as bad or unworthy of response, but, rather, because he was consistently responding to her deeper desire – her desire for connection, intimacy, spirituality.

The story of the woman found in adultery, in my retelling in Chapter 1, involves sexual tension and shows how we identify with and excuse romantic relationships. We understand why the woman and young man acted in the way that they did – because their love for each other, and their sexual entanglement, made a way for them to overcome boundaries of culture, fear and morality.

In both stories, Jesus is more concerned about the real inner people they are than in their sexual behaviour. In some ways, the women are good symbols of our society as they are making sexuality and romance a primary focus, yet nurturing a deep longing for spirituality underneath.

I am convinced that one of the reasons for the success of the bestseller *The Da Vinci Code*[12] (apart from it being a good yarn) is that it suggests Jesus was human enough to be sexual and allows a woman to share centre stage with him. Our society has a longing for a God who includes the feminine, is earthy and sexual and yet is still God. *The Da Vinci Code* was not doing away with Jesus as divine, although it was certainly questioning the Church's interpretation of him.

Over the centuries, the Church has had an uneasy relationship with sexuality, preferring either to ignore it or condemn it. The Bible, in contrast has been upfront about the ecstasy as well as the danger of sexual encounters. While the Song of Songs is the prime example of spiritual–sexual writing in the Bible, this theme is certainly also present in the writings of many of the mystics and is a metaphor often alluded to by the prophetic writings. The intersection of spirituality and sexuality has a long tradition in Christian writing, not just as a metaphor but also as a recognition of our embodiedness, our humanity. God chose to share in that embodiedness in the incarnation, the centrepoint of revealing himself to us.

Clearly, spirituality and sexuality overlap – they both have to do with our deepest longings, both have to do with true intimacy and both are about our greatest vulnerability. The purpose of each is to find another – another person or another being – and becoming truly open to them. The best of both sexuality and spirituality can be represented by the Garden of Eden phrase 'naked, and were not ashamed'.[13] The ideal is to be able to be naked before another person in sexual intimacy and not be ashamed of our nakedness and to be naked before God and not be ashamed of our naked transparency and our longing before him. God seeing us as we truly are and our not being ashamed of that is true spirituality.

My sexuality is an important part of my identity, part of how I relate, part of what energizes me. Some of us can accept that but then do not take the next step – bringing my sexuality into God's presence. Many people somehow try to leave their sexuality at the door of the church, leave it out of their prayers. In their chapter on sexuality and prayer, Ann and Barry Ulanov suggest why:

> Most things we leave out of our praying are things that frighten us, embarrass us, or make us ashamed. Sexuality needs to be faced and included in just those particular terms, with just those special variations that insist upon our individuality. God loves all of us, and therefore our sexual lives too. So we must bring to prayer the excitements, the wonders, the confusions and the bruises that make up our lives in this area, just as much as we bring the issues and problems of spirit and soul.[14]

In fact, our sexuality reflects the very core of being human. At one level, sexuality is a metaphor for our spirituality. It is a concrete image of what we are like in our deepest being. Henri Nouwen expresses it like this: 'Our sexuality reveals to us our enormous yearning for communion. The desires of our body – to be touched, embraced and safely held – belong to the deepest longings of the heart, and are very concrete signs of our search for oneness.'[15]

God created us to be in relationship and our sexuality pushes us to recognize that. I wonder how many of us would be hermits, or certainly unmarried, if it were not for sexual desire propelling us into relationships.

In reflecting on sexuality, it is important to recognize that it relates to the whole of our being – it is not just the sexual act of intercourse. It is part of the energy system of our being, it is present in all our relationships and, without it, we are quite mechanical or robotic. So much of story and film is intensified by sexuality, the sexual tension that draws people into relationships. In some ways, we have learned to think of this as bad or dangerous, but it is a God-created danger. It seems that God chose to take the risk of creating us as sexual beings, giving us an inordinate yearning for relationship, so that we would continually seek connection, spark off each other and return to the subject of relationship again and again. It is as though we needed something to propel us out of our self-centredness to participate with others.

Sexuality demonstrates to us that love is dangerous and creative, fulfilling and stripping, ever-emerging and challenging. Sexuality shows us the essence of relationship, that love is not a weakened 'being nice' or living in codependence, but wild and untameable, life-giving and demanding, insistent on honesty and self-giving. Neither sexuality nor real love allow us to stay safely in the false self. Both call us to grow beyond our safe boundaries, to be vulnerable and authentic.

David Schnarch,[16] a sex therapist, explains that the sexual relationship is a window on to how we relate at all levels. Because of the power of sex and our sexual urges, it exposes the reality of our relationship patterns, challenging us to be honest and grow. It illustrates for us how love is meant to be lived out, in authenticity, generosity and nakedness. It shows us the risk we take when we love – in fact, when we are truly human. As John tells us, 'The person who refuses to love doesn't know the first thing about God, because God is love – so you can't know him

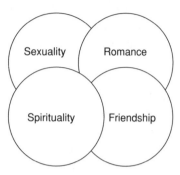

Figure 4
Four kinds of intimacy

if you don't love ... No one has seen God, ever. But if we love one another, God dwells deeply within us.'[17]

Our sexuality, then, is not only part of being human but also part of being created 'very good'. Spirituality and sexuality are very close together. Both are about intimacy, nakedness, being known. There are four spheres we may enter to find intimacy – sexuality, spirituality, friendship and romance (Figure 4).

These overlap each other and the core of each is intimacy and being known. Each also has traps – a fallen side. Sexuality, instead of being a desire to connect and give to another, can become an addictive self-indulgence. Romance, instead of finding beauty and poetry, seeing the best in the other person and the relationship, can become fantasy – an addiction to unreality. Spirituality, rather than finding intimacy with God, can become a legalistic, religious set of rules. Friendship can become a code-pendence instead of a mutual sharing of the inner self.

Viktor Frankl, a psychologist and survivor of the Holocaust, saw these dimensions of relationships as being more like layers. He saw the outermost layer as being the sexual level. The romantic, or erotic, penetrates more deeply 'into the psychic structure of the other person ... we are also "infatuated" with the other's psychic characteristics.'[18] He saw spirituality – loving the other person – as being the deepest layer: 'Loving ... alone penetrates as deeply as possible into the personal structure of the partner. Loving represents a coming to relationship with another as a spiritual being.'[19]

The story of the woman at the well could be read super-ficially as being about her looking for sex, but, in reality, we can see that she was seeking something much deeper. That is the subject of the next chapter. Her story is played out in many of our popular stories. The film *Pretty Woman* is just such an example of a story of sexuality and romance having become distorted and yet the deeper longing for connection being evident. Of course, the two leading actors, Richard Gere and Julia Roberts, are attractive and beautiful. It is not a realistic story – we understand that it is a myth. In the story, the pros-titute, ironically, recognizes the danger of making an intimate connection with the men she sells herself to. Her rule is to never allow the man to kiss her, seeing this as being too intim-ate. She has lost the true intimacy of sex yet has preserved the knowledge of something better. She longs for romance – for her prince to come on a white horse and take her away to a better place. The businessman who begins a relationship with her brings his own baggage – as a reaction to his anger at his father, he buys up and dismantles businesses. Only as he grad-ually begins to accept himself in the context of this increas-ingly real relationship is he able to explore his destructive behaviour. In such an unlikely setting, each is reaching out for the deeper desire – true connection and true selfhood.

Sexuality, and the metaphor that it is, can thus lead us to our deeper desire – to our longing for connection with God. Down the centuries, the mystics have frequently used the language of 'lover' and 'beloved'. The Song of Songs is a prime example. Teresa of Avila is known for her metaphors of the 'interior castle' and the 'spiritual marriage' as illustrating stages of the spiritual journey. Ulanov and Ulanov write, 'When we read the giants of prayer, we discover how frequently they include sexuality in their visions of God and in their metaphors and allegories of relation to God. The highly charged language of the Song of Songs is everywhere in their writings. The abiding rhetoric in Teresa of Avila and John of the Cross, Origen and Gregory of Nyssa, Bernard of Clairvaux and William of St Thierry, gathered from the Old Testament sources, is of sexual embrace.'[20] Julian of Norwich, a woman mystic, whom we encountered on page 80, wrote:

Truly our Lover desireth that our soul cleave to Him with all its might.

He is our clothing that for love wrappeth us, claspeth us, and all encloseth us for tender love, that He may never leave us.[21]

Men, too, use this kind of vocabulary. St John of the Cross wrote *The Spiritual Canticle*, which is very reminiscent of the Song of Songs. His *Dark Night of the Soul*, with its mix of genders, explicitly uses a sexual encounter as a metaphor for his encounter with God. I include the final verse:

I remained, lost in oblivion;
My face I reclined on the Beloved.
All ceased and I abandoned myself,
Leaving my cares forgotten among the lilies.[22]

Recognizing the parallel between sexuality and spirituality can open a door for us, enable us to bring all of our being into relationship with the Divine and see that our spirituality and our deepest hungers can find their fulfilment in God.

While sexuality, spirituality and romance can each lead us to that place of intimacy and openness, so can an awareness of our brokenness. As we have seen, Henri Nouwen noted that our sexuality and brokenness are often close together as our deepest needs often become sexualized. Acknowledging my body's desires and my romantic longings helps me to connect with my deepest longings for union and communion. It is in recognizing those deep longings and temptations that I find my place of need. My longing for intimacy, my longing to be desired by another, my looking to another person for love and affirmation – all of these point me back to my need for God: 'It is obvious that our brokenness is often most painfully experienced with respect to our sexuality. My own and my friends' struggles make it clear how central our sexuality is to the way we think and feel about ourselves. Our sexuality reveals to us our enormous yearning for communion.'[23]

Nouwen talks about 'bringing my body home'[24] – not the old idea of repressing our sexual urges, but making friends with them. A straightforward exercise can help to bring us in touch with these. We simply come to God in prayerful silence, consciously aware of our bodies, our sexuality, learning how to do this without shame by accepting that God sees our sexuality as very good. For some of us an exercise like this immediately makes us feel uncomfortable, even unclean, because often our sexuality is close to our woundedness, our brokenness. Often our shame keeps us from bringing that to God.

In facing his awareness of his own desperate need, Nouwen wrote spiritual imperatives to himself – and so to us. For example, 'Your body needs to be held and to hold, to be touched and to touch. None of these needs is to be despised, denied, or repressed. But you have to keep searching for your body's deeper need, the need for genuine love. Every time you are able to go beyond the body's superficial desires for love, you are bringing your body home and moving towards integration and unity . . . Thanks to the Incarnation, you can bring your body home.'[25]

Brokenness and sexuality both have to do with the most intimate aspects of myself – my vulnerability, my nakedness – and yet it is possible to be naked and not ashamed. Our calling is to find that we can be broken, we can be naked, we can be our true selves and need not be ashamed. Becoming aware of our own need and pain is a way to come more honestly into God's presence. In our society, this may be particularly difficult for those who are homosexual, especially if they have imbibed the belief that their sexuality is somehow evil or bad in itself. As a culture, especially the Christian community, we have contradictory beliefs about sex. We have scriptures that are upfront about sex, sexual temptation, sexual fulfilment, sexual sin, and our society is soaked in sexual images, but the Church certainly does not talk about all this openly and freely, apart from perhaps alluding to the dangers of sex and sexual sin.

From the very beginning, the Garden of Eden story makes it clear that we are sexual beings. Jesus referred to this in his answer to the Pharisees' questions about divorce being lawful for any and every reason. His answer, in a nutshell, was, 'Divorce is not God's idea. God's idea is that we are male and female and that we marry and become one flesh.'[26] The creation story, too, is forthright about the fact that we are sexual beings and being sexual is good. It is at the end of the story, after God has made them male and female and told them to multiply, that he looked on what he had made and saw that 'it was very good.'[27] Some cults have a twisted idea that the sin in the garden was a sexual one, but, interestingly, the Bible does not suggest any such thing – it sees the sexual relationship between Adam and Eve as good.

God could have made us angels, with no sexuality. He could have made reproduction occur as it does in the plant kingdom or made mating as brief as it is for most animals. He didn't. He gave us bodies that have eyes to enjoy visual beauty, ears to enjoy music, tongues to enjoy food and skin that enjoys being touched. He made us sexual beings and intercourse ecstatic. He created us with bodies and invited us to dance!

As I identify with Jesus' real-life peers, with their own sexuality, so I find the real Jesus who interacts with me. I acknowledge my own longing and my own fallenness. As I engage with this Jesus, I find that my longing, my desire, even my sexual desire, which I thought I must somehow hide, instead can lead me to him. When I am honest about my yearning, I can move forward to the deeper desire, to the God who created us as intimate, deeply yearning beings. I identify with the woman at the well and her use of her own sexuality as a way of trying to meet the deep needs of her being. Jesus would have heard her innuendo, but consistently responded to the true longing of her heart. He revealed himself to her, as he did to very few – and only when they were ready – as the Messiah.

16

The woman at the well

I see him sitting there. In the shade, still, watching.
I become conscious of myself, my body. I swing it a little.
I lower my bucket and glance at him. He meets my look and asks for a drink.
There is something in his eyes. Some promise of such richness. Forbidden, of course, but worth pursuing.
The old longing in my heart – the longing for someone who will meet me, the real me, fully.
There is no man, I know, who can do that, but I still hope.
I make a play for it. 'Who are you, a Jew, who would ask?'
I flirt a bit, draw him in, engage him.
I take him my bucket and pour water into his hands. He thanks me and drinks. I watch him. In his look is such self-containment, such a wholeness.
I know that he will not be tempted by me. He is not, yet he is not afraid to give.
He responds to me and lets the playacting fall away ignored.
He drinks and says, 'If you knew who I was you'd ask me for a drink.'
I'm asking, oh, I am asking, but how to meet that look?
So I continue my act.
'Well, give it to me, then I wouldn't have to come here and draw water.'
I draw him along, keep him talking.
On one level I'm not acting. I want this life he has in his eyes. I want to know how to get it.
I'm free for the taking, if he'd only have me, which he won't, of course. If he's as great as he seems, he'll see my broken-ness and not want me. He does see it – 'Go and call your husband.'
I'll try for a little longer all the same. 'I have no husband.' Take me, I'm free. I'll give you all that I've got for what you've got.

107

I'm yours for the taking and I'll give it all for that life you have in your eyes.

He knows what I mean. He looks at me deeply. He doesn't draw back from me. The promise is there in his hands. If only.

He looks at me and, without judgement, still holding out the promise, he says, 'You're right, you've had five husbands and the one you now live with is not your husband.' Statement: I know you.

So he knows my brokenness and my need. He sees through me and, wonder of wonders, does not draw back. Oh, if only I could have this man. Indeed, he would be living water to my soul.

I do not know how to get him. He plays a game that I do not know.

I'll try another tack to keep him within reach a little longer. 'Sir I can see you're a prophet.' Well, something. You're something to do with what my inner heart longs for. Talk about that. Tell me the answers – tell me something that I can feed on for a while.

He talks and I do not hear him. I watch his lips and his eyes and know that I long for something that is beyond my reach, physically and spiritually. I am one who longs for spiritual answers but cannot attain to them – who would even believe that I wanted them? I give myself physically to receive whatever life I can get, but this man, he knows something, he is in touch with what is real, it's not hard to see that. He takes me seriously. He talks to me as if I am someone who is real, too. He's not sidetracked by my banter.

He looks into my eyes and my spirit is drawn to him.

I dare to let him see my real longing. 'I believe in the Messiah.' I want to know him.

'I am he', he says.

I am stunned, yet believe, all in the same instant. I stare at him, my bucket forgotten, the men coming up behind me ignored. If anyone could be, it's him. He looks into my eyes. Gentleness and truth, the promise of life for ever, living water. It really could be true. I am caught in his look, caught by the promise. I am known for who I am, yet free to come.

I meet his look. My heart is held, yet free.

For once I can give my heart, freely.

My whole being says 'Yes'.

17

Shadow, brokenness and darkness

The woman at the well was a woman who knew her own brokenness and something of her own shadow. I have imagined her in many different ways. Perhaps she was a very broken, timid woman who came out at noon to get water because she knew that no one else would be there. The other women would have long ago taken their water for the day and then be in the cool of their homes, out of the midday sun. Perhaps Jesus' need for her to draw water for him gave her enough courage to talk with him. Maybe a man who gave her a second look and interacted with her as a real person was a rarity for her.

Maybe she was, in fact, a brazen prostitute, not caring who saw her out in the street in the middle of the day, jangling her bracelets, after her long lie-in. Maybe she was so tired of people's judgements and sidelong looks that she let herself be seen and came to the well when she felt like it, whoever was around and whatever strange men might be about. Perhaps her responses to Jesus were quite rude and aggressive: 'How come you, a Jew, ask me, a Samaritan and a prostitute, for a drink. Don't you know that it will dirty your hands to receive a drink from me?'

I have located my writing of her story in the previous chapter somewhere in between these two extremes. I have in mind that she is a woman who knows her own sexuality and is not afraid to use it in her relationships with men, hoping to nurture at least something of what her deeper self, her soul, craves in any kind of connection that she can create. So, I have imagined her flirting with Jesus, angling for any scrap of intimacy that she can pick up. On the surface she plays a game, but, underneath, her heart is longing, reaching out for relationship. Jesus always seems to have been on the lookout for hearts that are open – however well different kinds of games are played on the outside. To my way of thinking, he is able to see through her acting to the woman underneath. He can see beneath the hurt, the brazenness, the flirtation to the longing of her heart. So, he responds always at that level, to her heart's cry, undistracted by her superficial behaviour.

I see this woman as being one of the broken ones who come to Jesus more easily than those of us who are caught in the legal requirements of good behaviour and the false self. Her own conviction that she will never be acceptable according to society's standards enables her to sidestep the traps of the false self and walk into a relationship with God. She lets herself be seen for who she is and so is an example to us of how to come to God – in brokenness, letting our darkness be seen, admitting our fallenness.

The admission of fallenness is one aspect of accepting shadow – the part of myself that is devalued, maybe dark, unacceptable either to ourselves or to society, and therefore hidden away. Shadow can be defined as 'that which I do not wish to be, that within myself with which I least desire to associate, that which I find frightening, anarchic and threatening to my self-image.'[1] The false self is the part of us that wants only to project a good, acceptable self-image. The true self allows itself to be seen, warts and all, acknowledging the parts that others do not want to see. That is how I see the woman at the well – willing to let her need and her desire be seen, even if she uses her sexuality to do so. Her very willingness is what brings her into the presence of the Messiah. She could have just given him a drink and moved on, but her need was so great, her desire so immediate, that she let it be seen. It is hard for many of us to believe that the very part of us we do not want to recognize is the part that could bring us to the Messiah if only we will acknowledge it.

The shadow is not the 'sinful' part of us. Rather, it is the hidden, unacknowledged part. Robert Johnson, a therapist and author, explains the development of the shadow like this:

> somewhere early on our way, we eat . . . of the tree of knowledge, things separate into good and evil, and we begin the shadow-making process; we divide our lives . . . we sort out

our God-given characteristics into those that are acceptable to our society and those that have to be put away . . . But the refused and unacceptable characteristics do not go away; they only collect in the dark corners of our personality. When they have been hidden long enough they take on a life of their own – the shadow life.[2]

The shadow, then, is formed from God-given characteristics. Psychoanalyst Carl Jung said that the shadow is actually 80 per cent gold.[3] However, it consists of parts of us that we are uncomfortable with because our society or our parents or we ourselves thought they were not acceptable. If only we can hang in there long enough, stay with the uncomfortable long enough, and the anxiety, and acknowledge our own weaknesses and biases, we can find the gold hidden there. It is a very vulnerable place to be, though – a place of nakedness – and, because of our anxiety and past experiences, usually (at least initially), a place of shame. The woman at the well seems to have contended with a lot of her shame and this enables her to be seen for who she is, to stay with Jesus even when he speaks of her shameful past and present. Somehow, she was able to trust him enough and is desperate enough to let him see her, the whole of her. That is what we are called to – to live nakedly in grace. If I really believe that God is a God of grace – and grace is God's operating medium – then living nakedly is the best way to grow, to live knowing grace to be real. So it should be in my relationship with God – I need to come to him in nakedness, knowing that I am loved. Indeed knowing that I am loved, enjoyed, delighted in – that is the only way to come to him nakedly. Only as I develop in myself this sense of grace and extend it consistently to others will I be able to live out this vulnerability and freedom.

It is easier for us to think that we can come broken to God at a time of conversion or maybe at a crisis point or a time when we need to repent. As a place to live our lives from permanently – that is a different matter. Learning to accept that my shadow is a part of the ongoing person I am, that there are different parts of myself that are frightening, anarchic, threatening to the image of the person I would prefer to see myself as, is hard, but embracing the shadow is the only way to become whole: 'To honour and accept one's own shadow is a profound religious discipline. It is whole-making and thus holy and the most important experience of a lifetime.'[4]

There are various ways in which we can identify the shadow parts of ourselves. One of the most useful is to think about our dreams. Bible stories frequently cite dreams as a means of understanding something or hearing God's voice.[5] It seems that in biblical times there was an acceptance of the relevance of dreams and that God's voice could be heard through them. Research shows that sleep and dreaming are, indeed, a means of healing and regeneration.[6] We often dismiss dreams as absurd or meaningless, but their very absurdity is a key to their meaning.[7]

One of the basic principles – and one of the hardest to really believe – is that every character in the dream is you and characters of your own gender frequently represent shadow parts of yourself. Let me explain with an example. In my day-to-day relationships I am generally a loving and accepting person. I even pride myself on how kind and accepting I am, but, like everyone else, I have my own internal dialogue of criticism and evaluation that I do not want others to know about, don't want to even acknowledge to myself. In my dreams, there are various women – those I know and those I don't – who I am critical of or who are critical of me. Acknowledging that these women represent parts of myself is the key to interpreting the dreams, understanding what those parts of myself know and so being able to embrace them.

Let me give you an example. A while ago I dreamt that I had locked up a woman I know in a suitcase, starving her. On waking I tried to describe the woman. She was detailed, accurate, sharp and perceptive. In what way was I locking up those parts of myself, not listening to the parts of myself that are perceptive and accurate?

It takes practice, and often another person, to help us analyse our dreams in this way so that we can hear what they are telling us. The more I listen to people describing their dreams, the more astounded I am at our brains' creativity in helping us to acknowledge and understand parts of ourselves.

Many of us who have a Christian faith believe that we are to 'live in the light' and 'flee temptation'. That can set us up to believe we should not have a shadow side and certainly not 'embrace the shadow', 'embrace our own darkness' or get in touch with the pain. We have confused 'shadow' with 'evil' and believe that struggling with desire is a result of a lack of self-discipline or the need to die to the self. Shadow is much more complex and elusive and often has energy that we need, but, in fact, hold down and repress, denying ourselves access to it.

Another way to see our own shadows is to notice what we fight against in ourselves, what we 'forget' or what we resist. Learning to look at our resistance, even to go towards it, can help us find the gold. Noticing what it is that we keep putting off or what we 'forget' to do continually can be a key to identifying our own shadow.

Many people who are depressed, exhausted, emotionless discover that they are using a huge amount of energy to hide parts of themselves that they do not want to acknowledge or else repressing energy because it is associated with anger or fear or hurt. Some writers suggest that our shadow is a source of great energy, that the 'wild side' when it is acknowledged can bring us to freedom and vitality. Henry David Thoreau, a philosopher and activist whose writing influenced Tolstoy and Gandhi, contended that our shadow – or wild part – is to be valued as much as the good. This is something of a revelation for those of us committed to living – and helping others to live – 'good' lives. Thoreau writes, 'I found in myself, and still find, an instinct toward a higher, or, as it is named, spiritual life, as do most men, and another toward a primitive rank and savage one, and I reverence them both. I love the wild not less than the good.'[8] Here he is addressing the misunderstanding that the 'wild' is evil or savage in a destructive sense. He is trying to point out the energy in and the value of the 'wild' part of us, that it is worthy of reverence and just as much so as our more overtly spiritual side.

In order to comprehend and acknowledge the energy held in our shadow, we often need to experience it. Many of us intuit this energy but are afraid to explore it, aware of its possible destructiveness. Sexuality is an example of a high-energy part of us that we often keep strongly in check for fear of the possible consequences. We intuitively fear the destructive side of the Tristan and Iseult story happening to us. Yet, many of us have experienced the healing and relationship-building aspects of a healthy sexual relationship.

The energy of anger is another aspect of shadow that many of us do not know how to handle constructively and so repress. There is a huge amount of positive energy in anger, but most people have not learned to harness it for good. The idea that depression is 'anger turned inwards' is connected with the repression of anger that is so often associated with depression and the large amounts of energy that are used up to bury these strong feelings, as well as the destructiveness of this process. The willingness to explore their anger is often key to depressed people finding a way out of their depression as they can then tap into that hidden energy.

To believe that the shadow is 80 per cent gold, we often need to experience that to be true. To understand that it is possible to explore the shadow part of ourselves without letting it control us is a process of learning. One way to safely experience shadow is by engaging empathetically with someone else's story. Identifying with a story can help us to recognize the interwoven 'good' and 'bad' qualities of another person. Seeing the turning of a weakness into a strength in someone's life can demonstrate the alchemy of transformation. Wisdom stories, fairy tales and stories of our faith can be helpful here. Recognizing the weaknesses of the heroes in these stories can help us accept our own shadow.

The story of the very human apostle, Peter, is one of recognizing shadow, of his learning to use the energy he had to change things to have a positive effect rather than a destructive one. Many Old Testament stories are shadow stories – Abraham and his lack of faith, Joseph and his childish boasting, Gideon and his fear, David's sexual encounters. The story of the woman at the well is another as it shows the shadow of her overt sexuality and need, the acknowledgement of which leads her to have an honest encounter with the Messiah.

It is too easy for us to believe that shadow is somehow 'done away with' at conversion. We might think that the woman at the well would, from that encounter onwards, no longer experience that shadow part of herself as she had become a believer. In fact, we have to accept the more difficult idea that shadow and gift are intertwined. The part of us that has energy and creativity and constructive outcomes also has an unacknowledged or unwanted shadow side. The very fact that I am a loving, kind person means that I try to hide my more critical, perceptive side. For me, embracing that particular shadow involves learning to listen to my critical side and turning it around, using what it tells me to speak the truth in love to myself and others – a much more difficult challenge than simply trying to be 'nice'.

In the next chapter, I tell the story of John the Baptist as a means of exploring the implications of shadow and gift being part of the same package. I have imagined Mary, Jesus' mother, talking about her memories of him as a child and her perceptions of him as an adult. John was outspoken, confronted people and was very courageous. These characteristics were both gifts and partly shadow and were to be his undoing. His driving motivation was to set people right, to challenge them to repent and turn to God and live lives worthy of that repentance. I can imagine Mary pondering as to whether or not he could have acted differently, learned to speak out more circumspectly. That is the challenge that we all face – how do we live in a way that lets the energy of our gifts flow without it being destructive to myself or others?

18

John the prophet, John the Baptist

Mary, the mother of Jesus, tells the story of her kinsman, John.

As you can imagine, John always had a special place in my heart. 'John the Baptist' they call him these days, because that's what he became famous for. Of course, that's not what he is to me. He will always be just John, my favourite aunt's son, born in her old age, a precious pregnancy and life that I shared with her.

My first news of John did not come from Elizabeth – I did not even know that she was pregnant. How it all happened is still something that I hold dear in my heart, but I'm careful who I tell about it because not everyone believes in angels – they look at you differently ever after once you've said that, but you've asked me to remember everything as accurately as I can, so you're going to have to accept that angels are part of my story!

John's story started for me in the middle of a beautiful afternoon. I'd gone down to the stream – picking flowers, if I remember correctly. That was before I was married, still living at home with my parents. I helped my mother a lot in the kitchen, learning all I could so that I would be a good wife and mother, yet I still liked to go down the valley and dawdle beside the stream. It was a way to spend time with God too – to glory in the beauty of his creation and feel his presence in the sunlight and the trees, the sweep of the valley and the sound of the water babbling over the stones.

So, I'd sat down, then lain back, feeling the warm sun and looking up at the clouds, daydreaming, praying, just being in the beauty and presence of the Creator.

When I opened my eyes, someone was sitting beside me. He greeted me as if I was some high-born lady. I remember being confused – laughing at the thought of being mistaken in that way and yet somehow sensing his seriousness underneath and being a little afraid of what it was all about.

He told me that I was highly favoured by God. I had a child-like faith, I guess, in those days – that God delighted in us all – so I listened to what he had to say. He went right on to tell me that he had been sent by God, his name was Gabriel and, in the next breath, that I was going to have a son. Well, you know all about that, but, as if to reassure me that he was telling me the truth – or that miraculous things like this really can happen – he told me that Elizabeth was pregnant, even though she was old. In fact, she was in her sixth month. Well, he certainly thought of the right thing to tell me! I thought, Elizabeth will be just the right person to understand all this – she's my favourite person in all the world – and she will help me know what to do.

My mother didn't know what to make of my sudden request to go and see Elizabeth, but she trusted me enough to let me go and, fortunately, I was able travel down to her a few days later. I don't think I could have borne having to wait any longer. I kept going over and over what the angel had said – that I would bear a son and that Elizabeth was pregnant, too. I was so grateful that Elizabeth was pregnant, as well. Obviously her child was also someone special and I knew that she would help me to make sense of all this.

I have to say, I was a little afraid. What could it all mean? 'Son of the Most High ... Conceived by the Holy Spirit ... Sit on David's throne ...' yet my heart just kept singing. Elizabeth was pregnant, too!

By the time I reached her, I was ready to burst with the news – how good God is, how he uses the small things of the world to confound the mighty, the poor of the world to humble the rich, the ones who are of no account to bring to nothing the arrogant and the proud. I knew these things because he was using me – and Elizabeth.

She was in the kitchen when I burst in and, as I called out my greeting to her, I saw her face light up and her hand move imme-diately to her stomach, her robes curving gracefully over her preg-nant belly. 'Ah, Mary – favoured of the Most High God,' she said. I laughed – her words reminded me of the angel's. 'How is it that the mother of my Lord should come to me?' she said and we looked into each other's eyes and knew that we could trust each other with anything that we wanted to say.

I told her that I'd come because an angel had told me of her child and, as I hugged her, she laid my hand on her belly and together we felt the baby moving inside her. 'He leapt inside me the moment he heard your voice,' she said. That's how I first met John, moving in her womb in response to my joy.

I stayed with her until he was born – the light of her life and of her old age. Of course, I saw them as often as I could – our babies becoming toddlers and then little children. I watched John grow up. He was an unusual child – serious and deep. Children of older parents often are a bit different, but there was more to it than that with him. He took life very seriously. Of course, he and Jesus played together when we were there and, yet, often they'd seem to get into serious conversations instead of the usual games that children play. My other children would be off playing together somewhere and then we'd see two heads bent in conversation – John and Jesus on some deep topic. The questions they would ask! They were always at Zechariah to explain about the temple and the priests. Sadly, he died when John was still a child, but, before then, they'd be asking questions about God and about the commandments, the old stories and new interpretations.

John always had a bit of a sharp edge to him. He would see where people weren't living in the way that he thought they should. He would see things very clearly and call people to account, even as a child. Elizabeth would look at him sometimes with such a depth of love, but I think that maybe she guessed he wouldn't last long in this world – too outspoken, even as a child, that one. Jesus would question, too, but somehow he did it differently – made you want him to explain, somehow drew you into the discussion. With John, though, the sharpness felt almost like an accusation sometimes. It was obvious that he wouldn't become a priest like his father – questioned the system too much and, indeed, he had ideas of going away on his own even when he was young. So, when Elizabeth died, well, by then he was old enough to make his own decisions, look after himself. He'd already made it very clear that he was not going to marry, that he had been called by God to live a life apart. He'd never touched wine and at that point he chose an even more ascetic way of life. He wanted to have no part in the worldly systems around him at all. He was going to withdraw from the city and go and spend time with God, by himself, apart. I feared for him then. He obviously saw and understood things that few do, but he spoke out about it. I hoped that going away might teach him prudence. Well, prudence from my point of view – he might have called my prudence cowardice.

We didn't see him then for years. Occasionally we would hear a rumour that he'd become something of a holy man living in desert places. Jesus would become quiet when we heard anything of him. He'd see the concern on my face and reassure me, 'That's his way. He has to do what he has to do.' I'd remember what Zechariah and Elizabeth used to say about him, that Gabriel had told them he would turn the hearts of many towards God. I prayed that he would, that he would know how to speak to people to draw them to him.

When next we heard of John, Jesus had started to travel around the country. John certainly was drawing people – drawing crowds of people, by all accounts. When I was told how he spoke, I wondered at him. He'd indeed grown strong in spirit, very courageous, but, oh, how outspoken. He called all who came to him to repentance, to change, asking them to turn around their way of life. He spoke like the prophets of old. He called the people to live lives that were worthy of someone who had truly turned towards God. I was told, too, that the multitudes went out to him. It was good news, but, oh, I feared for his life.

Sometimes people would quieten when I came near if they knew that he was related to me, but I heard the talk anyway. 'You brood of vipers', he'd said to the religious leaders. Oh, John – always needing to speak out the truth as you saw it. Elizabeth would have been proud of you, but I was glad that she wasn't alive to hear this.

Certainly, he drew many to repentance. Many were baptized by him and many truly chose to lead a better life because of him. I wasn't surprised, though, when I heard he'd ended up in jail – for rebuking Herod, of all people. He hadn't learned to keep quiet around those in authority. He spoke the truth even to Herod. The wonder is that he didn't lose his life sooner. Herod kept him in jail for some time. He liked to talk to him, so the rumours had it. In the end, he still had him beheaded – at some whim of his stepdaughter's, so they said. Well, if it hadn't been that, it would have been something else. Too courageous by far, too outspoken, but then how can I say that? It was his gift, his calling from God and he fulfilled it. He lived life to the full in the way he saw fit.

I wonder sometimes if he could have done it differently. What would have happened if he had learned how to speak convincingly without bringing destruction on himself, if he could have lived longer and continued to influence our people and our nation, but he didn't. He lived as he thought he should, his sharp edges cutting at people's consciences. He made a lot of people think and, yes, I believe that he did prepare the way for people to hear about the kingdom, to hear Jesus' teaching as a whole new way of being and live in the kingdom with our God as father. I'm glad, though, that Elizabeth and Zechariah didn't live to see his imprisonment and execution. I prefer to think about how they would have been satisfied with the man he chose to be. They would have been proud of him, the joy of their lives.

19

Humility – being known for who I am, becoming who I am

———◆◆———

Mary's telling of John's story shows us that he was a man with unique gifts, that he had the energy to confront people deeply and he was finally executed in Herod's prison cell for his beliefs and being outspoken about them. Each of us has to find our own way through the challenges of the gifts we have been given, our motivations and energy and our particular shadow side. If we repress the shadow too much, we seem to dampen and even extinguish the energy that comes with our gifts. Yet, if we go too far into the shadow and the kind of energy it has, we can become self-indulgent or destructive.

It is usually much easier to see the shadow in other people's lives than in our own. It is the part of the other person that we simply find 'too much', too over the top. Yet, in ourselves, it is a drive that feels so right, that gives us energy and meaning. Learning to embrace the shadow is learning to find the gift and the meaning, turning it around so that it energizes us to serve others and live life to the full: 'We can't experience our gift in all its depth without at the same time discovering the dark and potentially destructive side of our gift.'[1]

I have imagined Mary telling John's story because it is easier for others to see our gifts – and our weaknesses – more objectively than we can. We hide our brokenness for fear of it being seen, but in doing so we also hide our beauty. It seems that the journey to the recognition of our true self and our real beauty is the same as that of exploring our shadow and acknowledging our weakness and brokenness. Only as I admit my failures can I also see my own beauty. Only as I disclose my own abilities and name them can I also own up to my weaknesses. Somehow these two sides of ourselves can be apprehended only if we are willing to see and accept both.

Many of us have believed that it is being proud to see our own gifts and strengths and therefore unacceptable. However, as we saw earlier, Henri Nouwen tells us that the greatest trap in life is not success, popularity or power, but self-rejection.[2] Marianne Williamson has recognized that truth, too: 'Our deepest fear is that we are powerful beyond measure. It is our light, not our darkness, that most frightens us . . . We are born to make manifest the glory of God that is within us.'[3] The very popularity of those words (often misattributed to Nelson Mandela), which tell us that our deepest fear is our power and light rather than our darkness, suggest that they ring true for many of us. There is something about our own gifts and abilities that frightens us, holds us back from acknowledging and using fully the best in ourselves and keeps us in a smaller life than the one we are capable of living.

C. S. Lewis' retelling of the myth of Psyche and Cupid, *Till we have Faces*, is a profound exploration of the true and false self, self-rejection and glory.[4] The story is told by Orual, Psyche's sister, who becomes queen. Although in many ways she is a good queen, she does not recognize her own goodness because she lives a life of regret (and self-justification) for how her actions banished Psyche. It is only in the last pages of the book that we read how Orual discovers her own beauty and see that, at a deeper level, Orual and Psyche are one and the same – beauty and innocence, wisdom and duty – different sides of the same human reality.

Orual's life journey is an allegory of our own – the long, slow journey of facing the best and the worst in ourselves and only finding the best when we finally also acknowledge the worst.

True humility is not hiding our gifts and strengths. True humility is being seen for who we are – gifts, strengths, weaknesses, self-justification, failures, shadow and glory. Peter's gift to us is that he showed us how to let it all be seen. As we appropriate this gift, we too are transformed, as Orual is in Lewis' story. That is true humility – the disclosure of who we are in order that transformation can happen. Many of us have thought that, if we are to dance with God, we must become nothing.

Maybe we have believed that we are to 'empty ourselves', in the sense of a total obedience that knows nothing of self. However, if Irenaeus is right and 'The glory of God is a person fully alive',[5] then God is glorified by our being real, whole people. The dance then takes on a whole new dimension as it is the dynamic between two complete beings rather than a dancer, God, and a ghostly shadow-partner, us. This is authentic living in the true self, the willingness to be open about who we are in order that we might change and grow.

If we live in the paradigm of the false self, the paradigm of evaluation, we are constantly measuring ourselves and others against some external criteria. Our relationships are also then shot through with evaluation and comparison rather than the freedom of discovering who we are at our best and creating space for others to discover themselves. In our relationships, we are brought into an 'over and against' position – measuring others against the requirements that we consider to be essential, requirements that may have developed from our own childhood scripts and bear no relation to what God intends for us (Figure 5).

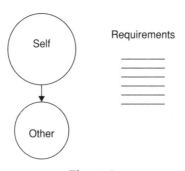

Figure 5
The self evaluating the other

Many Christians find themselves caught in this paradigm and so, in their relationships – whether they be in the form of friendships, discipling, mentoring, teaching – they feel bound to assess themselves and others against these requirements. Doing so places the self in a privileged position because

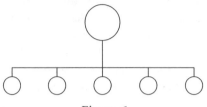

Figure 6
Hierarchical organization

we tend to measure others against our own internalized standards. Living by the law in such a way frequently leads to a hierarchical understanding of relationships because comparison and therefore ranking are implicit in that paradigm (Figure 6).

If we are to live as the true self, in the kingdom, we need to understand what that means for our relationships. We must live truly as brothers and sisters with mutual respect and acceptance. We need to find alternatives to hierarchy – to wanting a king to rule over us.[6] The kingdom is an alternative way to live in relationship with God and those around us. In telling us about the kingdom, Jesus invites us to a whole different way of being, to relationships where we see each other as equals and learn to value each individual and the gifts we each bring. It is true community and an alternative way of living and relating.

Scott Peck, in his insightful book on true community entitled *The Different Drum: Community-making and peace*,[7] explores the stages of relationship and community-making. He sees the first stage as being pseudo-community, which is when we are all nice to each other, but don't reveal too much, especially when we disagree. Relationships can operate at this level in a rather civilized way, but we are not intimate and we cannot grow.

The next stage is called chaos. That is because we start to be more real with each other. Peck says that we try to 'heal, fix and convert'[8] each other, creating chaos and the breakdown of relationships. Many people retreat to pseudo-community at this point to escape the discomfort of chaos. However, the only way through it to the final stage of true community, which is real relationships, is to go through the stage Peck calls emptiness. That entails a letting go of the desire to fix, heal and convert.

As I have used these concepts to make sense of my own relationships, I have become more aware of my desire to remain in control of them by doing exactly that – fixing, healing and converting. If I can make the other person more like me, I will be more comfortable with them. That is certainly not true community, nor is it having respect for the other.

At some point, we all resist the efforts of other people to fix us. If we don't, then it is likely that we are giving them too much authority over our lives. We each are called to become our true selves in relationship with our Creator, to work out our own salvation.[9] That does not mean we cannot receive input from others, of course, but we are to retain responsibility for our own growth and we are to allow others to have that same responsibility.

The stage of emptiness, then, in our relationships is when we let go of the urge to fix, heal and convert others. Instead, we become willing to simply accept them as they are and walk the journey with them as fellow human beings. Even in my relationships with others as a counsellor, spiritual director or teacher, I am to walk the journey alongside them. That is the way to live as the true self in our day-to-day relationships (Figure 7).

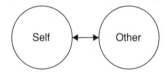

Figure 7
The self and other in equal relationship

If the paradigm of evaluation is our mindset we will have great difficulty walking side by side with others, accepting them as they are. If, however, we truly embrace the way God relates to us, in utter grace and acceptance, then we can extend that grace and acceptance to others. The meaning of the name of the Holy Spirit is 'the one who walks beside', in Greek the *Paraclete*.[10] God himself chooses that kind of relationship – walking beside us. It is the outworking of the spirituality of descent – God emptying himself to become one with us,[11] to walk beside us. That is true humility, a willingness to be seen for who I am and

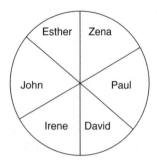

Figure 8
A different model of organization

choose to see you as you are, with respect and acceptance. The outworking of this pattern within organizations is for there to be a commitment to equality. That does not mean each person has to have the same role, but people's gifts and roles are given equal respect (Figure 8).

Such an understanding of working together fits with Paul's various metaphors for the body of Christ working together organically: 'God has arranged the parts in the body, every one of them, just as he wanted them to be. If they were all one part, where would the body be? As it is, there are many parts, but one body. The eye cannot say to the hand, "I don't need you!" And the head cannot say to the feet, "I don't need you!" '[12]

Christ is to be the centre, we are to relate to each other as brothers and sisters, differently gifted, and grow up into maturity through our relationship with Christ, individually and jointly (Figure 9). There is to be no other mediator between each of us and God.[13]

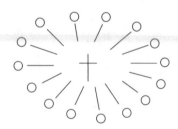

Figure 9
Relating, in equality, to Jesus

To talk in such a way is not to talk about organizational effec-
tiveness, but about the quality of our relationships and our
responsibility to relate directly with God, not allowing others to
stand between God and myself. In the kingdom, God alone is
the king and we are each his subjects and his lovers.

That is actually a much more challenging way of relating than
is hierarchy, which is why we so often revert to hierarchical
relationships. Relating together as equals requires more commitment to honesty, openness and vulnerability – truly living in the
kingdom here and now. One of the major challenges of this way
of relating is that of learning to speak the truth in love. That is
the way, Paul says, we will 'in all things grow up into him who
is the head, that is, Christ.'[14]

If I am to speak the truth in love, I have to learn to truly direct
my heart towards other people. That is the challenge of living in
the kingdom. If I harbour judgement – coming from resentment
or hurt or superiority – my heart will not be truly 'for' others,
I will be living instead in the paradigm of evaluation, trying to
fix, heal or convert. To come to true community, to be truly for
the other person, I must come by the way of the cross, the way
of emptiness, which is that of accepting others as they are. That
is the deepest challenge of living in love as we are confronted by
our own need to change. As John has told us, 'if we love one
another, God dwells deeply within us'[15] and 'For anyone who
does not love his brother, whom he has seen, cannot love God,
whom he has not seen.'[16]

John, in his old age, worked out what the essence of kingdom
living is. It is that we are to love and, in so doing, God will dwell
in us and we will live a Christlike life, living the kingdom. That
is not pseudo-community as other people will intuit if we are
false, if we are judging or fixing. There are no shortcuts to
'truthing in love',[17] as the Greek wording has it. The only way is
to constantly allow God to show us the behaviour and attitudes
that hold us back from being truly for others. Living the truth
in love demands that we engage in a constant process of transformation with the God who delights to see us dance in the freedom of our true selfhood.

20

Ongoing transformation – engaging with the self-revealing God

We are called to walk the narrow way[1] – that is the way of trans-formation, the way that leads to life, the way of choosing love for our fellow travellers. Jesus' stories are full of pictures of living in the kingdom. Paul's letters are full of exhortations to grow up into maturity. Of course, there are many ways in which we grow and develop into living more fully as sons and daughters of God. Growing in intellectual understanding is one way. Emotionally identifying with the stories of our faith is another way. The stories contained in this book have been included to aid your emotional understanding and growth in your relationship with God. Many of us have not learned this particular way to practise being in the presence of God, to discover the richness of experiencing the reality of Jesus.

Jesus calls us to 'Love the Lord your God with all your heart and with all your soul and with all your mind and with all your strength.'[2] In fact, he is quoting – or, some might say, misquoting – Deuteronomy, where it says, 'Love the Lord your God with all your heart and with all your soul and with all your strength.'[3] The word 'mind' was added to the New Testament version, emphasizing that we are to use our minds as we love and serve God. Note that he is also emphasizing that we are to love God with our hearts as well – with our passions and our emotions. The Jewish idea of the person was more holistic than ours. The Greek influence somehow separated mind and heart, but Jesus emphasizes both.

In the last few centuries, the West has privileged rational knowing – that is, intellectual head knowledge has been seen as the highest form of learning and our educational systems have, similarly, emphasized rationality, evidence-based learning and scientific method. More recently, a balance has been occurring, with an exploration of 'emotional intelligence', as well as a return to valuing intuition and 'connected knowing.'[4] The English language does not help us to make distinctions between these ways of knowing as we use the word 'knowing' for all of them. However, French (and many other languages) distinguish between knowing a fact, *savoir*, and knowing a person, *connaître*.

Cultures that have not chosen to privilege rationalistic thought as much as we have in the West understand religious stories much better than we do. They are more practised at hearing religious and mythical stories on a deeper, less literal level. Christians also do it to some extent. When we talk about 'living in the promised land' or 'killing the Goliaths' in our lives or trusting God to keep us safe from the fiery furnace or the lions' den, we are using our faith stories to help us live well in our ordinary lives. That is what religious stories are for and they are passed from one generation to the next to continue to help us understand the way life is and how to feel God's presence in our lives.

Most of us do this to some extent, but not as richly as we might. We also get caught up in applying a principle purely at a head level, rather than letting it enter our hearts and change us from within. While applying a principle does help us to use scripture in our lives, it often lacks the deeper transformative element. The biblical understanding of the word 'to know' is less intellectual, much more relational, more intimate than head knowledge. God is calling us to this intimate, interpenetrating relational sort of knowing – an intimate relationship with a God who knows us intimately and loves us beyond all understanding. Bernard Lonergan, a philosopher theologian, in exploring levels of learning and knowing, reinstated relational knowing as being at the peak of human consciousness.[5]

One of the important ways in which we can open ourselves to God's transforming touch is to use this kind of knowing to enter the stories of Jesus' life and interactions with those he met. Putting ourselves holistically into the stories of Jesus allows us to experience his presence, his invitation to live in relationship with him, his invitation to dance.

The stories included in this book of the woman found in adultery, the woman at the well, the man with the shrivelled hand and the woman who washed Jesus' feet, the stories of Mary, Peter, John and Paul all serve to illustrate how to do exactly that. They are stories in which I have tried to stay true to the biblical text, but have used my imagination to fill in the gaps. The woman found in adultery is the most obvious example of this. I am not proposing that what I have written is the real story as it actually happened. Rather, I am imagining a possible story that enables me to identify with her, to come emotionally to the feet of Jesus, as it were, and so experience his response. That is a far more powerful way to read the story than to merely read the words. Too often, people get sidetracked into debating, for example, the morality of the story, emphasizing that Jesus told her to 'sin no more', or questioning what Jesus was writing in the sand. Instead, I find the part of myself that truly feels as the woman would have felt and, when I bring that hurting, guilty, sad, angry part into Jesus' presence, healing takes place. Approaching the woman's story in this way enables me to enter the story and bring a part of myself into relationship with God, in the present, experience God's grace as she did, gain understanding of Jesus' risk in standing up for me, in finding a way of forgiveness for me. In the process, my heart is drawn to him and I want to follow him and become like him.

To appropriate the story for myself, I have imagined how I could have somehow got myself into this woman's position. The exact process for doing that will be different for everyone. You can ask yourself questions about it. How might I have been tempted? How might I have fallen into sexual sin? How might I have been pushed to that place? What are my areas of vulnerability? I find that, as I answer these kinds of questions, possibilities arise and I can more easily imagine – and so identify with – the woman in the story. As I do so, I experience the response of God-become-man – to me. Thus, I experience God's forgiving grace healing the most vulnerable parts of myself.

The story of the man with the shrivelled hand developed rather differently. I imagined myself as that man, just as I have written. There was no lead up to his story, simply the question of what would it feel like to be that man. I bring in what I know or believe to be true of the culture of the time. I remember other stories where someone's sickness causes questions to be asked about who sinned, that it is punishment for doing something to displease God.[6] So, imagine this man, struggling with his obvious disability and believing that others will see his lack of healing as a sign of him receiving God's judgement for some wrongdoing. As I imagine him struggling with the shame of that, I notice the experience of shame in my own life. Thus, when I imagine the man encountering Jesus and Jesus' initiative in healing him, I experience it as his reaching out to me, his willingness to come looking for me and my shrivelled places. Somehow, the process of identifying emotionally with the character facilitates the experience of encountering the real living Jesus in the present – and my own hurt and shame are healed as part of that.

It is a safe way to release and experience our imaginations and emotions. It does not involve fantasizing or 'making up' how God reacts to me as I am staying close to the accounts of Jesus' real-life interactions in the Bible. How does he respond to a woman found in adultery? How does he respond to a man born blind, his culpability in question? How does he respond to a woman married five times and now living 'in sin?' I am not inventing how I would like him to react, but reading what our sacred writings tell us and so discovering the God revealed in human form.

As I see his reactions to the woman found in adultery, the woman at the well, the woman who washes his feet with her tears, I am also challenged by his responses to the other characters in the story. The Pharisee part of me is confronted by his challenge to be as forgiving as he is. The self-justifying, arrogant part of myself that would condemn others is challenged to look at my own weaknesses, my own sin, my own lack of generosity of grace to others. Not just my head but also my heart is provoked to let go of judgement and forgive as I have been forgiven. Doing that is a transformative process that changes me.

Another way to enter a story is to get in touch with an area of struggle or an emotional reaction in yourself. That is how I came to write the story of Peter. I was struggling with accepting myself as being imperfect, not living up to my own standards, wanting to present a façade of wholeness. As I got in touch with that feeling, I recognized my need to bring it to God for transformation. I tried to stay with that feeling, the awareness that I did not have it all together, that I could tell others what I believed was the right way to live and yet fell short of it myself and so had failed to live out what Jesus had been teaching me.

Focusing on the experience of the emotion helps you to go to the story that is most relevant to your situation. The question I ask myself is, 'Who in the Gospels felt like this?' Very often, a wonderfully relevant story will come to mind. Who in the Gospels became aware of their failure, who in the Gospels had to admit their imperfection, had to let Jesus see their weakness? They are not intellectual questions so much as heart questions. As I feel the emotion, I let it guide me to a person who also felt like that. Then, I can experience the reality of my emotion and the reality of Jesus' response. Thus, when Peter heard the cock crow and realized that he had indeed fallen short of his own conviction, his own honest desire to please Jesus, and I imagine Jesus turning and looking at him, I too experience the tears of self-revelation. Also, when, out of that experience of self-recognition, I too admit to Jesus that I fall short of what I want to be like in loving and serving him, with Peter I experience the grace of the one who continues to call me to follow him, the one who comes to me where I am and gives me a task in his kingdom. The emotional experience of the encounter continues to change my heart and deepens my walk with the one I want to love more dearly, follow more nearly.

I wrote Mary's story in a similar – but opposite – way. I was recognizing my tendency to feel that I should deserve God's love, that somehow I need to be worthy of God being a loving parent to me. As I asked the question, 'Who else felt like that?', Mary's story came to mind – not because she too felt like that, but because, in fact, she epitomized the opposite of that feeling. She knew that she didn't deserve God's favour yet did, simply because God is a God of grace who delights in using the lowly, undeserving ones.

At first, I found her story difficult to write because she exemplified the very experience that I was struggling to achieve myself.

So, I wrote the story initially as if Elizabeth was telling it. Elizabeth told of Mary visiting her, 'hurrying up the hill as though the glory of God was about to burst on her'. Then I imagined what it must have been like to be inside Mary's skin – a village girl, who could somehow accept the favour of Almighty God. I imagined how Elizabeth might have described her. Elizabeth must herself have wondered if God disapproved of her and that was why she was barren. I imagined Elizabeth recognizing Mary's childlike acceptance of God's presence. That helped me to go to the childlike place in myself that also knows the wondrous cherishing of God. Then I found that I could tell Mary's story as a fourteen-year-old girl might have experienced it and, having found that girl in myself, I was more able to get in touch with the part of myself that can accept God's love innocently, simply, as a child might. I understand more of what Jesus meant when he said that we can only enter the kingdom of God as a child.

One of the ways in which you can engage with a story imaginatively and emotionally is to tell it as if you were one of the characters in it who is telling a friend or writing in a diary. The more details you include, the more real you make the scene. To do that is to follow the instructions of Ignatius of Loyola of the sixteenth century on how to 'pray the Gospels.'[7]

Ignatius encouraged his followers to imagine the story and become very aware of their senses – what they could see, hear, touch, smell. What was it really like to be there? Because I am someone who is often more aware of my inner world than the outer one, I emphasize being aware of the emotions. What would the person be feeling? What would it be like to experience Jesus in that way? The fact that each person who tells the story will tell it differently does not matter. The point is to engage personally with the story. What would it be like for me to be in the story – as an onlooker, as a disciple, as the key person, even as Jesus?

Sometimes it is helpful to imagine the story from different people's points of view, as that highlights different parts of yourself – the repentant part, the Pharisee part and so on. It is a good way to encounter shadow parts of yourself, parts that you would not initially identify with, but somehow recognize and process when you find them in someone else's story. The prodigal son and his older brother is a wonderful story to analyse in such a way. Henri Nouwen has demonstrated the process in his deeply insightful book *The Return of the Prodigal Son*.[8] He identifies with the prodigal, the older brother, the waiting father, each in turn. In doing so, he recognizes the contrasting parts of himself and uses the story to lead himself more deeply into the arms of the waiting heavenly Father, as well as to become a father to those he worked with.

The most successful books, stories and films are those we can identify with – we are literally 'moved' by engaging with the main character in each one. We are changed afterwards because, for a short time, we have walked in their shoes, experienced their lives. The process of praying the gospels enables us to be moved by God, to be transformed and a little more like the Christ we encounter there.

My hope is that the stories I have told in this book will inspire you to engage with the gospel stories in your own new way. I hope, too, that you will encounter the Jesus of these pages experientially and engage deeply with your own journey of relationship with the Divine, finding the one your soul longs for. *Maranatha*. Come, Lord Jesus. Come, that we may dance with you.

Notes and acknowledgements

Introduction

1 D. Ladinsky, from the Penguin publication *The Gift: Poems by Hafiz* (New York, Penguin Compass, 1999), p. 270. Copyright © 1999 Daniel Ladinsky and used by his permission.
2 Matthew 11.28–30 (RSV).

1 The beginning of the story . . .

1 John 8.3–11.

2 The inner life – the kingdom within

1 Matthew 5.17–20.
2 John 18.36.
3 Matthew 7.3–5 (RSV).
4 Proverbs 4.23.
5 John 17.11, 16.
6 Matthew 6.33.
7 Ecclesiastes 3.11.
8 Rainer Maria Rilke, 'Ich leibe dich, du sanftestes Gesetz', 22.9.1899, Berlin-Schmargendorf, my translation from original German text, available at <http://rainer-maria-rilke.de/ 05a025sanftestesgesetz.html>
9 J. A. Sanford, *The Kingdom Within: The inner meanings of the sayings of Jesus* (San Francisco, Harper, 1987).
10 Matthew 23.25.
11 Luke 16.15 (*The Message*).
12 John 8.3–11.
13 From Clare of Assisi, 'he was born poor he died poor', in C. M. Ledoux (C. J. Dees trans.), *Clare of Assisi: Her spirituality revealed in her letters* (Cincinnati, St Anthony Messenger, 2002), p. 109.

3 The man with the shrivelled hand

1 Matthew 12.9–14.

4 True self and false self

1 D. W. Winnicott, *The Maturational Processes and the Facilitating Environment* (London, Hogarth, 1965), cited in M. Davis and

D. Wallbridge, *Boundary and Space: An introduction to the work of D. W. Winnicott* (New York, Brunner-Routledge, 1981), p. 48.

2 D. Ladinsky, from *I Heard God Laughing: Renderings of Hafiz* (Walnut Creek, California, Sufism Reoriented, 1996), p. 127. Copyright © 1996 Daniel Ladinsky and used by his permission.

3 Luke 15.11–31.

4 Luke 7.37–50.

5 M. B. Pennington, *True Self False Self: Unmasking the spirit within* (New York, Crossroad, 2000), p. 46.

6 Pennington, *True Self False Self*, p. 49.

7 Rainer Maria Rilke, 'Wir dürfen dich nicht eigenmächtig malen', 20.9.1899, Berlin-Schmargendorf, my translation from original German text, available at <http://rainer-maria-rilke.de/05a004eigenmaechtig.html>

8 Luke 18.9–14.

9 Luke 18.9 (*The Message*).

10 Luke 18.10–13.

11 Luke 18.14.

12 Luke 16.15 (*The Message*).

13 For example, H. J. M. Nouwen, *In the Name of Jesus: Reflections on Christian leadership* (New York, Crossroad, 1989).

14 Matthew 4.1–11.

15 Pennington, *True Self False Self*.

16 Nouwen, *In the Name of Jesus*.

17 Matthew 4.8–9.

5 Gratitude and the true self

1 Matthew 11.29 (*The Message*).

2 World Values Survey, 1991–2001, discussed in article by M. Bond, 'The pursuit of happiness', *New Scientist*, 4 October 2003, issue 2415, and reported on BBC News, available at <http://news.bbc.co.uk/2/hi/africa/3157570.stm>

3 Luke 7.37–50.

4 Matthew 6.2, 5, 16 (NKJV).

5 Luke 6.17–26.

6 Matthew 5.3.

7 John 5.39–40.

8 Rainer Maria Rilke, 'Du siehst, ich will viel', 22.9.1899, Berlin-Schmargendorf, my translation from original German text, available at <http://rainer-maria-rilke.de/05a014ichwillviel.html>

9 Meister Eckhart c. 1260–1327/8.

6 Knowledge of good and evil

1 James 1.23–25.
2 Romans 7.19, 24.
3 I first heard this phrase from Gary Hayachi, from a Living Waters seminar.
4 Genesis 2.9.
5 John 5.19.
6 John 8.28.
7 John 14.20.
8 Romans 8.1–5.
9 Matthew 7.12; 22.36–40.
10 Acts 5.30.
11 Genesis 3.5.
12 Luke 18.9 (*The Message*).
13 Philippians 2.12.
14 Genesis 2.25 (RSV).
15 B. J. Sims, *Servanthood: Leadership for the third millennium* (Boston, Cowley, 1997).
16 Exodus 20.1–17 (RSV).
17 Galatians 3.24–25.
18 Galatians 4.4–7 (RSV).

7 Paul

1 Galatians 1.1.
2 Acts 22.3.
3 Philippians 3.5.
4 Acts 22.3 (RSV).
5 Acts 26.4–5 (RSV).
6 Galatians 1.13–14 (RSV).
7 Acts 26.9–11 (RSV).
8 Acts 5.35–39 (RSV).
9 Acts 6.11 (RSV).
10 Acts 6.13–14 (RSV).
11 Acts 8.1.
12 Acts 2.14–36.
13 Galatians 3.13; Deuteronomy 21.23.
14 Acts 22.4–11 (RSV).
15 Acts 9.9 (RSV).
16 Hebrews 8.13.
17 Jeremiah 31.31–34; Hebrews 8.8–12.
18 Matthew 26.28; Luke 22.20.
19 Galatians 1.11–12 (RSV).

20 Galatians 5.3.
21 Acts 15.1.
22 Galatians 2.2–5 (RSV).
23 Romans 2.28–29 (RSV).
24 Galatians 2.16, 21 (RSV).
25 Genesis 17.9, 13–14.
26 Galatians 2.11–12.
27 Galatians 3.24 (RSV).
28 Galatians 3.21 (RSV).
29 Galatians 5.18.
30 Galatians 5.1.

8 The crucified Messiah – a God of descent

1 Philippians 2.6–8 (RSV).
2 Mark 8.29–33.
3 Mark 9.33–37.
4 Mark 10.37.
5 Luke 9.54.
6 Luke 22.25–27.
7 G. N. Cosby, *By Grace Transformed: Christianity for a new millennium* (New York, Crossroad, 1999), p. 28.
8 Cosby, *By Grace Transformed*, p. 29.
9 Revelation 5.4–6.
10 Colossians 2.15.
11 Cosby, *By Grace Transformed*, p. 30.
12 M. Ross, *Pillars of Flame: Power, priesthood and spiritual maturity* (San Francisco, Harper & Row, 1988), p. xvi.
13 Ross, *Pillars of Flame*, p. 72.
14 B. J. Sims, *Servanthood: Leadership for the third millennium* (Boston, Cowley, 1997).
15 Cosby, *By Grace Transformed*, p. 31.
16 Nolan, cited in Sims, *Servanthood*, p. 16.
17 John 13.3–4 (RSV).
18 Sims, *Servanthood*, p. 17.
19 Sims, *Servanthood*, p. 17.
20 John 6.68.
21 Sims, *Servanthood*, p. 48.
22 Sims, *Servanthood*, p. 58, quoting Revelation 13.8 (KJV).
23 Matthew 27.46.
24 G. K. Chesterton, *Orthodoxy: The classic account of a remarkable Christian experience* (Colorado Springs, Shaw, 1908/2001), p. 145.
25 Ross, *Pillars of Flame*, p. 135.

9 Learning the path of descent – Peter's story

1 Luke 22.24–30.
2 Mark 9.33–37.
3 R. Rohr, *True Self False Self*, tape series (Cincinnati, St Anthony Messenger Press, n. d.).
4 John 21.15–17.
5 2 Peter 1.16.
6 The Greek word is *agape*, which means self-giving, unconditional love.
7 The Greek word is *philio*, meaning brotherly love or friendship.
8 D. Ladinsky, from the Penguin anthology *Love Poems from God: Twelve sacred voices from the East and West* (New York, Penguin, 2002) p. 65. Copyright © 2002 Daniel Ladinsky and used by his permission.
9 For a thorough exploration of this idea, see H. J. M. Nouwen, *Life of the Beloved: Spiritual living in a secular world* (Sydney, Hodder & Stoughton, 1992).

10 Mary's story

1 Luke 1.46–55.

11 Imperfection – the human condition

1 M. Leunig, *A Common Prayer* (HarperCollins (Australia) PTY Ltd, 1990, 1998). Reprinted by permission of HarperCollins.
2 D. Ladinsky, from the Penguin anthology *Love Poems from God: Twelve sacred voices from the East and West* (New York, Penguin, 2002), p. 306. Copyright © 2002 Daniel Ladinsky and used by his permission.
3 J. O'Donohue, *Anam Cara: Spiritual wisdom from the Celtic world* (London, Bantam, 1997) p. 151.
4 M. S. Peck, *The Different Drum* (New York, Simon & Schuster, 1987), p. 69.
5 Matthew 5.48.
6 See R. Young, *Young's Analytical Concordance to the Bible* (Peabody, Massachusetts, Hendrickson, 1984).
7 Luke 6.36.
8 B. J. Sims, *Servanthood: Leadership for the third millennium* (Boston, Cowley, 1997).
9 E. Arnold, *Salt and Light: Talks and writings on the Sermon on the Mount* (Robertsbridge, East Sussex, Plough, 1977), p. 7 (copyright 2004, used with permission from the Bruderhof Foundation, Inc.).

10 H. J. M. Nouwen, *Life of the Beloved: Spiritual living in a secular world* (Sydney, Hodder & Stoughton, 1992), p. 70.

11 Nouwen, *Life of the Beloved*, p. 27.

12 Nouwen, *Life of the Beloved*, p. 28.

13 G. M. Hopkins, *Poems and Prose of Gerard Manley Hopkins* (New York, Penguin, 1971), pp. 30–1.

14 Hopkins, 'That Nature is a Heraclitian Fire', *Poems and Prose of Gerard Manley Hopkins*, p. 66.

15 J. W. Fowler, *Stages of Faith: The psychology of human development and the quest for meaning* (New York, HarperCollins, 1995), p. 198.

16 M. Longley (ed.), *Louis MacNeice: Selected poems* (London, Faber and Faber, 1988), p. 70.

17 B. Manning, *Abba's Child: The cry of the heart for intimate belonging* (Colorado Springs, Navpress, 2001).

12 Surrendering what people think – the only way to true relationship

1 Genesis 2.18.

2 Proverbs 30.15.

3 Julian of Norwich *c.* 1342–*c.* 1413, *Revelations of Divine Love*, p. 55, available at <http://www.ccel.org/ccel/julian/revelations.html>

4 Frances Havergal (1874).

5 Mark 10.17–22.

6 W. Dych, *Anthony de Mello: Writings* (Maryknoll, New York, Orbis, 1999), p. 90.

7 W. J. Byron, *Jesuit Saturdays* (Chicago, Loyola, 2000), p. 4.

8 Luke 12.25.

9 D. Ladinsky, from the Penguin anthology *Love Poems from God: Twelve sacred voices from the East and West* (New York, Penguin, 2002), p. 163. Copyright © 2002 Daniel Ladinsky and used by his permission.

13 The deeper desire

1 R. Rohr, *Enneagram II: Advancing spiritual discernment* (New York, Crossroad, 1995). Also, see R. Moore and D. Gillette, *King, Warrior, Magician, Lover* (San Francisco, HarperSanFrancisco, 1990).

2 Job 42.3, 5 (RSV).

3 W. Johnston (ed.) *The Cloud of Unknowing and the Book of Privy Counseling* (New York, Image, 1973), p. 182.

4 J. Ruffing, *Spiritual Direction: Beyond the beginnings* (New York, Paulist Press, 2000), p. 11.

5 P. Yancey, *What's so Amazing about Grace* (Grand Rapids, Michigan, Zondervan, 1997), p. 70.

6 Ruffing, *Spiritual Direction*, p. 12.
7 Ruffing, *Spiritual Direction*, p. 13.
8 D. Ladinsky, *I Heard God Laughing: Renderings of Hafiz* (Walnut Creek, California, Sufism Reoriented, 1996), p. 131. Copyright © 1996 Daniel Ladinsky and used by his permission.
9 Ruffing, *Spiritual Direction*, p. 106
10 H. J. M. Nouwen, *The Inner Voice of Love* (New York, Image, 1998), p. 26.
11 Luke 6.20.
12 S. Weil, *Waiting for God* (New York, Putnam, 1951), p. 210.
13 J. Eldredge, *The Journey of Desire: Searching for the life we've only dreamed of* (Nashville, Thomas Nelson, 2001).
14 Rainer Maria Rilke, 'Du siehst, ich will viel', 22.9.1899, Berlin-Schmargendorf, my translation from original German text, available at <http://rainer-maria-rilke.de/05a014ichwillviel.html>
15 Song of Songs 8.5.
16 R. A. Johnson, *We: The psychology of romantic love* (San Francisco, Harper, 1985), p. xi.
17 Johnson, *We*, p. xiv.
18 Johnson, *We*, p. xiv.

14 Tristan and Iseult

1 J. Bédier (H. Belloc trans.), *The Romance of Tristan and Iseult* (London, George Allen), pp. 48–9.
2 M. Arnold, *Tristram and Iseult* in *Selected poems of Matthew Arnold* (London, Macmillan, 1852/1889).
3 J. Bédier (H. Belloc trans.), *The Romance of Tristan and Iseult*, p. 177.
4 M. Arnold, *Tristram and Iseult*.
5 R. Sutcliff, *Tristan and Iseult* (London, The Bodley Head, 1971), p. 134.

15 Romance, sexuality and spirituality

1 R. A. Johnson, *We: The psychology of romantic love* (San Francisco, Harper, 1985), p. xiii.
2 Johnson, *We*, p. xiii.
3 Johnson, *We*, p. xi.
4 Johnson, *We*, p. xii.
5 R. A. Greer (trans.), *Origen: An exhortation to martyrdom, prayer and selected works* (New York, Paulist Press, 1979), p. 223.
6 D. C. Downing, *Into the Region of Awe: Mysticism in C. S. Lewis* (Downers Grove, Illinois, Intervarsity Press, 2005), p. 62.
7 2 Samuel 13.1–2 , 6, 11–12, 14–15.

8 Song of Songs 1.2, 4, 15 (RSV).

9 Ephesians 5.31–33.

10 R. Sutcliff, *Tristan and Iseult* (London, The Bodley Head, 1971), pp. 7–8.

11 Sutcliff, *Tristan and Iseult*, pp. 60–1.

12 D. Brown, *The Da Vinci Code* (New York, Doubleday, 2003).

13 Genesis 2.25 (RSV).

14 A. Ulanov and B. Ulanov, *Primary Speech: A psychology of prayer* (Atlanta, John Knox, 1988), p. 76.

15 H. J. M. Nouwen *Life of the Beloved: Spiritual living in a secular world* (Sydney, Hodder & Stoughton, 1992), p. 70.

16 D. Schnarch, *Passionate Marriage: Love, sex, and intimacy in emotionally committed relationships* (New York, Norton, 1997).

17 1 John 4.8, 12 (The Message).

18 V. Frankl (R. and C. Winston trans.), *The Doctor and the Soul* (New York, Knopf, 1965), p. 134.

19 Frankl, *The Doctor and the Soul*, p. 135.

20 Ulanov and Ulanov, *Primary Speech*, p. 73.

21 Julian of Norwich, *Revelations of Divine Love*, The First Revelation, Chapters 6 and 5 respectively, available at <www.ccel.org/ccel/julian/revelations.ii.ii.html>

22 St John of the Cross, Prologue, Stanzas of the Soul, 8, *Dark Night of the Soul*, available at <www.ccel.org/ccel/john_cross/dark_night.vi.html>

23 Nouwen, *Life of the Beloved*, p. 70.

24 H. J. M. Nouwen, *The Inner Voice of Love* (New York, Image, 1998), p. 19.

25 Nouwen, *The Inner Voice of Love*, pp. 19–20.

26 Matthew 19.4–5.

27 Genesis 1.31.

17 Shadow, brokenness and darkness

1 J. Hollis, *Creating a Life: Finding your own individual path* (Toronto, Inner City Books, 2001), p. 119.

2 R. Johnson, *Owning Your Own Shadow* (San Francisco, Harper, 1993), p. 14.

3 Johnson, *Owning Your Own Shadow*.

4 Johnson, *Owning Your Own Shadow*, Introduction.

5 For example, in the New Testament alone, Matthew 1.20, 2.13, 19, (Joseph); Matthew 2.12 (the wise men); Matthew 27.19 (Pilate's wife).

6 E. L. Rossi, *Dreams, Consciousness, Spirit* (3rd edn) (Phoenix, Zeig, Tucker & Theisen, 2002).

7 There are a number of useful books for understanding dreams, such as J. Sanford, *Dreams: God's forgotten language* (San Francisco, Harper, 1989).

8 H. D. Thoreau, *Walden, or Life in the Woods* (New York, Vintage, 1991), p. 170.

19 Humility – being known for who I am, becoming who I am

1 R. Rohr and A. Ebert, *Experiencing the Enneagram* (New York, Crossroad, 1992), p. 8.
2 H. J. M. Nouwen *Life of the Beloved: Spiritual living in a secular world* (Sydney, Hodder & Stoughton, 1992), p. 27.
3 M. Williamson, *Return to Love* (New York, HarperCollins, 1992), p. 165. Although these words have frequently been attributed to Nelson Mandela's inaugural speech, they are not present in any of his speeches.
4 C. S. Lewis, *Till we have Faces: A myth retold* (Grand Rapids, Michigan, Eerdmans, 1964).
5 Irenaeus, *Adversus Haeresus*, Book IV, Chapter 20, 7.
6 1 Samuel 8.5–9.
7 M. S. Peck, *A Different Drum: Community-making and peace* (New York, Simon & Schuster, 1987), p. 86.
8 Peck, *A Different Drum*, p. 91.
9 Philippians 2.12.
10 John 14.16. The Greek word *Paraclete* can be translated as comforter, counsellor, helper, intercessor, advocate, strengthener and standby. *Amplified Bible* (Grand Rapids, Michigan, Zondervan, 2001).
11 Philippians 2.5–7 (RSV).
12 1 Corinthians 12.18–21.
13 1 Timothy 2.5.
14 Ephesians 4.15.
15 1 John 4.12 (The Message).
16 1 John 4.20.
17 Ephesians 4.15.

20 Ongoing transformation – engaging with the self-revealing God

1 Matthew 7.14.
2 Mark 12.30.
3 Deuteronomy 6.5.
4 See M. F. Belenky, B. M. Clinchy, N. R. Goldberger, and J. M. Tarule, *Women's Ways of Knowing* (New York, Basic Books, 1986).
5 B. Lonergan, *Insight: A study of human understanding* (New York, Philosophical Library, 1958).
6 For example, John 9 – the man born blind.

7 There are many books that can guide you on performing this kind of meditation. See, for example, S. Pritchard, *The Lost Art of Meditation: Deepening your prayer life* (Milton Keynes, Scripture Union, 2003).

8 H. J. M. Nouwen, *The Return of the Prodigal Son: A story of homecoming* (New York, Image, 1994).